A PLACE TO BEGIN

TEXT BY *Hal Borland*   PHOTOGRAPHS BY *B. A. King*

SIERRA CLUB BOOKS   SAN FRANCISCO   1976

A Place to Begin

THE NEW ENGLAND EXPERIENCE

Library of Congress Cataloging in Publication Data

Borland, Hal Glen, 1900-
    A place to begin

    1. New England—Description and travel—1951-
I. King, B. A. II. Title
F10.B67   917.4'04'4   76-21312
ISBN 0-87156-182-4

The Sierra Club, founded in 1892 by John Muir, has devoted itself
to the study and protection of the nation's scenic and ecological resources—
mountains, woodlands, wild shores and rivers. All Club publications
are part of the nonprofit effort the Club carries on as a public trust.
There are some 50 chapters coast to coast, in Canada, Hawaii and Alaska.
Participation is invited in the Club's program to enjoy and preserve wilderness
everywhere. Address: *530 Bush Street, San Francisco, California 94108.*

Printed in the United States of America.

For Barbara Dodge Borland
and Judith Stoddard King,
deep-rooted New Englanders
who have done their loving best
to make proper Yankees-in-law
of their outlander husbands

2

CHAPTER I

I USED TO THINK OF HOLLYHOCKS when I thought of New England. That was before I married a New Englander and came here, to the northwest corner of Connecticut, to live. I have lived here longer than anywhere else in my life, and though I came as an outlander I now call this home and I find my welcome here. But when I look out at our dooryard I see no hollyhocks. Phlox and iris and day lilies and lilies of the valley, but no hollyhocks. We had them when we first came here, in the perennial bed out beside the road; but the blight and the Japanese beetles did them in. We replaced them once, but the replacements didn't last. I had to settle for the memories of my first look at New England.

I had worked as a daily newspaperman over much of the West and South and had settled for a time in Philadelphia. My second summer there I decided to see what New England was all about. On my vacation I drove to New York, up the Hudson River to Kingston, then turned east. Soon I was in upper Connecticut and lower Massachusetts, some of the most beautiful areas in the East. And in every dooryard, beside every stern-faced farmhouse, were hollyhocks, their pleated, silken petals magnificently red and white and pink in the blazing sunlight of mid-July.

I saw other traditional things, too. The white churches, with and without spires. The cool village greens, with the famous New England elms. (This was before the elm blight killed so many of those beautiful trees. That blight is still virulent. Last year it killed seven elms along the half-mile road frontage of our farm.) And the classic old houses, most of them white and clapboarded. I had seen copies of those houses in Ohio and Indiana, in Kansas, even in Oregon. Here were the originals. I have been told that some of those in Oregon were laid out, cut, and fitted, practically prefabricated, here in New England, then shipped around Cape Horn to transplanted New Englanders.

I saw the big old barns with their vertical siding, aged to silvery gray and never touched by a paintbrush. And the small fields—mere patches, in the rural terms with which I grew up in the West. A few acres of corn here, a few acres of timothy just down the valley, a rocky hillside pasture—it seemed almost a travesty to call this farmland. And trees, which I supposed constituted woodlots. I knew the word, but had never seen a woodlot. There were trees on the hillsides above those patchy little fields, trees in the valleys, along the streams. And there was a brook or a river in almost every valley.

So this was New England—patches of corn, oats, hay, trees; rocky hillside pastures; brooks; white houses, gray barns. And hollyhocks.

I came to this corner of Connecticut that a few years later was to become home to me, and I conceded that it had its charms. But I still was bemused by miles and acres. The whole of Connecticut wasn't a great deal bigger than the county in Colorado where I grew up. All New England, for that matter, was smaller than the one state of Colorado. That was hard to believe when I looked at maps of the different regions. They were drawn to different scales, but that didn't show at first glance. Later, when I thought of going to see someone all the way across Connecticut from me I thought in terms of Colorado, which is almost 300 miles wide, north to south and more than 400 miles east to west. Connecticut is less than 100 miles west to east, about 60 miles north to south.

I went north across Massachusetts, angling toward New Hampshire. There, avoiding major highways, I met New England farm folk for the first time. I bogged down in mudholes on those back roads and had to find help to get out. That was before tourists had become a commodity. I was simply a stranger in need of help, and those farmers gave it generously, then offered hospitality. My farm background provided an unexpected link—I knew how to milk a cow, to harness a horse, to shell corn for the chickens. Our vocabularies were different, but we spoke the same language. I didn't feel at home, but I did feel welcome

I went on to Maine, which was a whole new experience, an area dominated by trees, by pines and hemlocks. An area of lakes and streams. Of rugged coves and headlands washed and battered by a cold Atlantic. I saw but learned little of Maine on that trip. Then I came south again, cut across the corner of New Hampshire into eastern Massachusetts. And from there, went down past Rhode Island, through southern Connecticut, across the Hudson to New Jersey, and back to Philadelphia.

It wasn't until then that I knew why some things I had seen in New England were almost familiar, as though I had been there before. I had, in a way. I had known New England in my boyhood, out there on the high plains of Colorado. It happened through a magazine, now long vanished, that was published in Boston. It was *The Youth's Companion*, and among its contributors was C. A. Stephens. I didn't know then and I don't know now, but it seems Mr. Stephens must have been a New Englander from way back. And he was a prolific writer. His stories appeared in the *Companion* every few weeks and I read them all, fascinated. He wrote about Morgan horses, ox teams, old stone walls, butternuts, Yankee people. He must have loved butternut fudge. I can still remember the way he made my mouth water for it.

I read *The Youth's Companion* because my father owned a country newspaper and because rural weeklies were often run in part on the barter system. Local people sometimes paid their bills with apples or potatoes or pork chops or dressed chickens. And the *Companion* bartered a year's subscription to the magazine for a small advertisement run in my father's newspaper a few times every fall. If *St. Nicholas* or *The American Boy* had made similar offers, I might have read them early, too. But they didn't.

The Stephens stories were typical *Companion* tales, strong on local color and weak in plot. Many of them were no more than elaborated anecdotes or character sketches. But they had flavor and richness. A few years ago I found a collected volume of Stephens' stories and tried to read it. It had no glow, no particular character, seemed contrived and shallow. I put the book aside, never opened it again. But the memories I already had made me smile with quiet pleasure, the way I did when I first read a volume of Robert Frost's poetry. And now and then I still meet somebody with a turn of phrase that makes me smile the same way, though I have been a New Englander almost thirty years. Once in a while Barbara, my Yankee-born-and-bred wife, says something, usually a quote from her father or her grandmother, that does the same thing, thanks to C. A. Stephens.

After Philadelphia I moved to New York to work on *The Times*. The nearest I got to New England was an occasional visit to Stamford or New Canaan or Westport, which are essentially suburbs of New York City. Then I quit daily newspaper work and we bought a few acres and a house near Stamford. A few years there—now I know it actually was a time of adjusting to the fact that we no longer needed to be within commuting distance of the city—and we decided to move on out. We considered going west, to Colorado or Arizona, but first I wanted to look at upper Connecticut. We came and we found what we wanted, a farm with riverfront, valley land, mountainside, and enough acreage for privacy. A house that would take our gear and provide room for two writers, a village only a few miles away, the nearest neighbor a farmer a half-mile down the valley. We bought it and moved in. Through Barbara, I already was a kind of Yankee-in-law. Now I became a resident New Englander.

I make a distinction here. Technically, the Stamford area is in New England. But practically, as I've said, it is a suburb of New York City. Our Salisbury area is out of commuter range, a hundred miles north of the city. It is not Old New England and it is not "the hinterlands," but there are old traditions here, old houses, old families. When we came here in 1952, several farmers still kept and used work horses in their fields. Oxen were used here as draft animals as late as 1910. Incidentally, they were called *cattle*, not *oxen;* the term, I have been told by men who know, was *a pair of cattle,* not *a yoke of oxen.* Now the cattle are milk cows, Holsteins and Guernseys. And though there are dozens of horses in the area, all of them are saddle horses.

This farm was self-sufficient, in the old, traditional way, for many years. The families that lived here kept milk cows, grew their own beef, made their own butter. They grew hay and corn to feed the livestock, which of course included work horses. They had a big vegetable garden and a special potato patch. They had a big orchard, mostly apples. Those who owned it just before we came here thought the apple trees had outlived their usefulness and had the orchard cut down, leaving about a dozen apple trees along the back yard fence and four pear trees in the far corner of what became the home pasture. The trees they left standing provide all the jelly and applesauce we can use, and occasionally they have a profuse year and are loaded with fruit we can't even give away.

At one time, they also grew tobacco here. Old-timers can point out where the tobacco barn stood and describe the work of growing tobacco. They still grow tobacco over to the east, in the Connecticut River Valley, shade-grown tobacco, and the netting used to shade it is like a gray fog hanging low over the fields. The tobacco barn here is long gone, but the big cow barn still stands. I had it reroofed a few years ago simply because I don't like to see an old, handcrafted building go to pieces from neglect. This is one of the really old barns, with oak and chestnut beams, hand hewn and pinned together, and faced with vertical siding of native pine that is now seamed and silvered with age and weather. There are few such barns left.

Earlier residents kept chickens and probably ducks, with the river so close by. There was a rambling chicken house with a good cement floor. I cleaned it out and put my power tools and workbench there, made it a shop for repairs and minor construction jobs that always demand attention on a country place. A small brooder house was perfect for storing lawn and garden tools. An old milk house near the road had already been converted into a garage. Just back of the house, a few steps from the kitchen door, was the woodshed, which had a privy in one corner for emergencies.

The house itself had cesspool plumbing and running water from a springhouse halfway up the mountain. Eventually we added a well, to take over in mid-summer when the spring ran low and the water had "a taste."

We put down the well the old, back-country way. First we cut a hole in the concrete floor of the basement. It seemed stupid to put the well in the dooryard, then pipe the water into the house, when we could have the well right in the house to start with. The Yankee man-of-all-trades who was helping me said, "Never saw it done before, but it makes sense." So we cut the hole in the cellar floor, then got four-foot lengths of 1½-inch pipe, threaded at both ends. We got a driving point, a conical brass fitting, perforated to admit water, and we screwed it to one end of a section of pipe. We made a driving maul from a short oak billet fitted with a handle, and we drove that pipe with its point into the ground where we had cut the hole in the floor. Length by length, we added sections of pipe and drove them on down. Less than twenty feet and we struck water, all the water we could use. An electric pump, a small pressure tank, a few new pipes, and we had a dual water system.

Driving a point is a simple way to get a shallow well, unless you strike rock. Here in our valley there is less than a foot of topsoil, then a foot or so of sand brought in by the river and washed down from the mountainside, and then gravel left by the glaciers. The topsoil is the accumulation of several thousand years.

The house was a square, two-story farmhouse with a porch all across the front. Two brick chimneys provided stovepipe outlets in each of its original eight rooms. Instead of being clapboarded, as it would have been in the village, its walls were shingled, like the roof, with cedar. Those shingled walls, we found, provide winter quarters for countless ladybird beetles. In late autumn and early spring they emerge on sunny days, some of them inside the house. We don't welcome them in our coffee, but we are glad to have them in the garden, where they eat thousands of aphids.

I didn't ask, but thought the house moderately old, maybe a hundred years;

interesting but not important. Then we met a daughter of the man who built it, and she said it dated only from 1917. But it was built from old, more or less standard farmhouse plans. The owners before us took out one downstairs partition to make a big living room and they somewhat modernized the kitchen. We made a few changes, none of them structural. It still is a mid-nineteenth-century farmhouse.

Lumber for the house was cut here on the farm. Cut and sawed with a portable sawmill. That, I am told, was common practice. Oak and chestnut were used for framing, chestnut for interior trim and stairways, native pine for sheathing. I can still find three good-sized piles of sawdust from the mill on the mountainside, now mouldered black and overgrown with bushes. The chestnut stumps up there still defy time and weather, though most of the pine stumps rotted away years ago.

We first saw this place in June. We had set out that morning to see this corner of New England, to see if it was where we wanted to live. We came north, taking our time, hesitating at several places, going back to look again. Early afternoon and we came to a place where the road skirted the west side of a long ridge, and off to our left, across a broad valley, was a range of hills like old, worn-down mountains. Beautiful hills. And the whole area seemed to open up. The valleys were broad and the hills gently sloped, there were trees but no dense woodlands, and there were two good-sized ponds in hollows perhaps a mile away, each one full of clear blue sky.

I stopped the car and we sat and looked. I said, "I like this." Barbara nodded. "Yes." She had never been in this part of Connecticut. I said, "I could work here. Live here."

We drove on, came to a village, saw the sign of a real estate dealer whose name we liked. Some people don't believe in hunches. I do. We told him what we wanted. A small, contemporary house and a few acres on a lakefront. He took us to three lakefront places, old, slightly moldy, smelling of mildew. We said no. Then he brought us to "a farmhouse with half a mile of riverfront." To this place.

He let us keep the key to the house, so we could come back later and look again, and he left. "He trusts us," I said. Barbara said, "He's a shrewd Yankee. He hopes we'll sell ourselves." We drove up the road, down the road, to the village. Late afternoon and we came back to the farmhouse. Its rather large lawn hadn't been mowed in two weeks, at least. We sat down in the grass, just to feel the good earth, to see if it welcomed us.

Orioles in the big sugar maples just across the road began to brag about the nests their mates had woven. A brown thrasher in one of the apple trees began telling us,

3

twice-over, that a thrasher can out-sing any oriole. A catbird came over from the riverbank to see what was going on, hid in a lilac bush, and chattered at us in several different languages, then jeered at himself.

We lay back in the grass and I looked into the blue depth of sky I hadn't seen in years. I felt the welcome from both sky and earth. I felt like making the Indian kinship signs to the four directions. Finally I sat up. "Want to go inside again?"

Barbara mentally placed our furniture. "No fireplace," I said. "We'll make the Franklin stove a part of the deal. No stove, no sale." We went upstairs, decided which room would be her study, which one mine. Both looked out across pastureland to the mountain, the woodland. Trees on a slope that lifted the eyes.

Then we went outdoors, down the front walk to the road, across the road to the riverbank. The Housatonic, a slow, placid river at this point, clear enough that we could see the bottom. A row of big sugar maples stood between the road and the river. I, who grew up in dry-land country, could scarcely believe we could own such a riverbank.

"I'll swim," Barbara was saying. "Miles." A swimmer, she loves water. Then she laughed. "Remember what we were looking for? A small, contemporary house with a few acres, on a lake!"

We locked the house, went to the motel where we had taken a room. The next morning we had another quick look, more or less routine. We were talking of it as "our place" by then. We stopped at the agent's office to leave the key and to tell him to draw up a contract of sale. Then we went home to Stamford.

We moved the last week in July. We had late summer here, then autumn. I thought I knew autumn in America. I had seen the incredible gold of aspens spilling down Rocky Mountain valleys with the maroon of scrub oak leaves for accent. I had seen maples and sassafras, scarlet oak and beech in the October woodland of Pennsylvania. I had followed the changing colors up the Appalachians from Carolina to the Lakes. But I had never seen a New England autumn.

It has now become my habit to speak of it in the laconic terms of New Englanders and simply say, "the Color." Every time I really try to describe it, I get up to my knees in superlatives. But I'll try again.

Autumn starts with the sumac, sometimes in mid-August. Staghorn sumac, inconspicuous all summer at country roadsides and in neglected fields, turns red, fiery red. A few branches at a time, then whole shrubs. The sumac fires start the fires in the swamp maples. They begin to glow, and the glow engulfs a few trees and then becomes a tide that floods a whole valley with soft-maple red, bright as cherry juice, bright as ripe apples.

Virginia creeper, which some know as woodbine, is inconspicuous in the woodland green until now. It climbs dead elms, festoons them all summer. Then it senses autumn, or sees it in the sumac and the soft maple, and it turns crimson and scarlet. The creeper is like sumac fire climbing those dead elms, giving them a spectacular beauty they never had when alive. Nearby is poison ivy, climbing trees and bushes or being a creeper or even a shrub, and it turns red and orange with an oily look to the three-part leaves.

The ash trees turn blue—white ash, that is; black ash turns conventional tan. Those blue white-ash leaves are gray in certain light, dark green in other light. Elusive. But they turn tan and yellow after the blue phase. And the birches turn a particularly brilliant yellow. Then come the sugar maples, late to color but not as late as the willows. The sugar maples first turn a simple yellow with no special glow; then the yellow deepens and in some seasons some trees take on shades of pink and even red. The yellow *ripens* — there is no other word. It becomes rich, deep, almost brassy; or it turns plain, full-color golden.

Then all those spectacular leaves begin to fall and the oaks come into their own with unpredictable crimsons and maroons and tans and purples. And the leather shades, particularly apt on those leathery leaves. By then October is fading into November. But while it lasts, the Color is special.

We saw the Color start in our valley that year, and we drove up into Massachusetts and lower Vermont and New Hampshire, then back through the hill-country brilliance. And when we came up our own valley we said, "This is best of all." And so it was. Perhaps not to outlanders, perhaps not to impartial travelers, but to us it was and still is best of all.

Thanksgiving came and went without one snowflake, perhaps indicating the degree of change in climate since Lydia Maria Child wrote the Thanksgiving song about the sleigh ride to grandfather's house. "Over the river and through the woods, etc.," written somewhere around 1850. Winter came with a snowstorm in mid-December and with cold that froze a ten-foot shelf of ice along both banks of the river. We had a white Christmas.

Spring came as usual in New England. It came on a mild afternoon in late April and stayed till sunset. It came again on a bright May morning and stayed all day. Spring, we were told, is a sometime thing. You don't plant beans until danger of frost is probably past, at the end of May. You don't set out tomato plants till Decoration Day. Only a couple of years ago we had a hard frost on June 6. But by June our neighbors are cutting hay, first cutting. Then it's summer.

Mid-summer and we had been here a year. I thought I had begun to understand New England. I hadn't. I never shall, completely. But enough so we could look about, travel some, talk, listen, and not be total strangers. Another two or three years and I would be ready to say I knew something about this area where we live. Now it is more than twenty-four years and I still don't know things a New Englander is born knowing. But I can set down some of the things I have learned.

4

8

9

CHAPTER 2

GEOLOGICALLY, New England is one of the oldest land areas on earth. The upthrust that formed the remote ancestors of the Berkshires and the Green Mountains heaved from the ocean depths half a billion years ago, during Cambrian times. The original upthrust was worn down several times, but some part of it remained above water through all the convulsions that shaped this continent. It was squeezed and wrinkled, twisted and warped, finally overlaid with lava from volcanos and from cracks in the tortured earth where the molten rock spilled out. It was worn down by flowing water and all the other forces of erosion. When the great convulsions ended, this area was almost a flat plain. Only here and there, particularly in the north—in Maine today, for instance, and in New Hampshire and Vermont—were there persistent snags of old mountains, tough rock that resisted erosion. Here in Connecticut, just up the rural road from where I am writing now, one cluster of gray limestone and white quartzite knobs still marks remote beginnings. The peaks are wracked and battered, eroded by water, scarred by ice, but still defiant of time.

Then, toward the end of the Cretaceous period, when the Rocky Mountains were being thrust higher than today's Himalayas, this whole New England area was lifted again, this time with little warping or twisting. The rivers cut deeper channels through the old valleys, leaving ridges and rugged hills of old volcanic rock still evident in the rolling terrain of much of New England.

This stage of erosion was still quite young when the Ice Ages began, about a million years ago. They began with a slight drop in temperature all over the world, three or four degrees, and with a slight increase in rainfall. High, cold areas such as northern Canada got a few inches more snow than usual and the snow lay on the ground a little longer each year. It began to accumulate faster than it melted. For decades, then for centuries, it piled up until it became glaciated, compressed into ice that would move of its own weight down the valleys. It squeezed out in all directions and began to flow southward. It became an ice sheet that eventually covered all of New England, much of the Middle West, and the northern part of the Great Plains. The ice became so thick—a mile or more in places—that it covered mountaintops.

As it moved across the land, the ice acted like a gigantic bulldozer. It crushed and gouged everything in front of it—trees, plants, soil, rocks, everything movable. And as it crept on and on, it tore out great chunks of bedrock and gouged great furrows in the earth. It carried a freight of rocks and soil from the uplands to the lowlands, filled old hollows, ground down old hummocks.

The Big Ice covered all New England, every inch, and swept the land clear. Then it melted back whence it came. Then it came again, in a few more thousand years, and melted back once more. This happened at least three times. Then, approximately twelve thousand years ago, for reasons nobody yet understands, another weather change moderated temperatures a few degrees. The ice no longer advanced. Its southern edge began to melt. The melting spread and the ice was eaten away from the top downward, so that mountains and hilltops were cleared first. The Big Thaw continued and the combined water from thaw and rain streamed down every slope. Rivers surged through every valley. Some valleys were still choked by orphaned ice dams and became huge lakes. As silt and debris accumulated in such lakes, the ice melted, the water drained away, and level tracts of stone-free land were left—areas known today as *plains* and highly valued by New England farmers. On some uplands the ice simply melted and loosed the load of earth and rocks it had carried for years. Even today the land shows such vast moraines, rubble of rocks and gravel that may be anywhere from a few inches to many feet thick. We call this *till,* and often a hole for a cellar or a cut for a road will reveal what a jumble of sand, gravel, clay, and rocks of all sizes (some even as big as houses) was left by the melting ice.

Most of New England's lakes and ponds were formed at this time, some by the gouging of the Big Ice, some by dams formed of debris dropped when the ice melted, some in huge hollows where fragments of the ice sheet persisted, somehow protected while the big melt continued. At least two of the small lakes here in my own area are definitely of glacial origin, and both are much deeper than normal for such small bodies of water, lending offhand proof to the slow-melt theory.

When the last of the glacial ice had melted, the land here was naked of plants and uninhabited by animals. This was true of similarly glaciated areas all over this continent, and in Europe and Asia as well. But the native plants that had been destroyed had persisted, with few exceptions, just south of the ice line. The ice, surprisingly, had not greatly altered the climate even a few miles from the front. It created fog and a degree of chill along the front, but that did not change the weather enough to kill the native plants. So when the melt-back came, the plants were at hand for a return of vegetation. Pollen counts show that even while the ice was disappearing the tundra plants, mostly grasses and sedges, but also plantain and fireweed began to grow again. Then, as soon as the ice was all gone from an area, the trees began to come back, mostly spruce and fir at first, with alders, willows, and some of the heaths.

When the climate had warmed up a few degrees more and the soil had improved a bit, another group of trees began to move in—hemlock and white pine, and such northern hardwoods as maple, birch, and beech. These are the trees that still clothe much of New England's upland.

I wish I had been here to see these things happening. But apparently nobody human was here. We have no testimony from witnesses. All we have is rocks and sand and scratches on the hills, and layers of pollen in the peat bogs. They tell what we know of the story.

As the climate moderated still more, the returning trees, which had retreated to the cooler parts of the Alleghenies during the Ice Age, moved still farther north and made room for a group of trees that had been evolving in the southern Appalachians—tulip trees, basswoods, chestnuts, sugar maples, sweet buckeyes, red and white oaks, hemlocks. And birch, black cherry, ash, red maple, sour gum, black walnut, and several species of hickory.

The land again was covered with vegetation, some of it with distinct southern origins, since plants always are restless and the changing climate became even warmer than it had been before the Big Ice. Some of this southern flora still persists, along the coast of southeastern Connecticut and eastward into Maine. Among these plants are holly, southern white cedar, rhododendron, and inkberry. Also, perhaps just to keep life interesting, poison sumac, one of the few especially painful irritants for the human skin.

The climate continued to change, but with its usual deliberation. After the ice melted, the temperatures continued to rise, reaching a maximum approximately five thousand years ago, judging by fossil remains and pollen counts in ancient bogs. Then the warmth eased off again. But for the past century it has been rising slightly. Some observers believe we are in an interglacial period. I would agree, and I think we are now beyond the mid-point, now are moving toward the Big Ice again. Here in New England we have had a series of mild winters and an excess of moisture, but up where the massive glaciers originate they have had colder winters with their excess of snow and rain. . . . But I am not going to debate this matter now.

The Ice Age not only changed the face of New England, it brought the first men to America, people whose descendants would populate this continent, to some degree, long before the first Europeans were even aware of its existence. By evidence we now have, these primitive men had come north out of Africa into Asia. There, some turned west and eventually reached Europe, where they would be known in our era as Cro-Magnons. Others, migrants and hunters, had turned east along the foot of the ice sheet. They followed the herds of musk oxen, woolly mammoths, long-horned bison, and horses. The herds grazed their way across a broad land bridge between Siberia and Alaska that was revealed when the vast ice sheet locked up enough water to lower the oceans' depth by as much as 300 feet.

They came, these primitive, nomadic people, and found a continent waiting to be explored and settled. They scattered down the length of it and across its breadth in the next few thousand years. Some went to South and Central America and evolved the cultures of Peru and Ecuador and Yucatan. Some went to Mexico and there created the Aztec culture. Some, in present-day Colorado, New Mexico, and Arizona, built the cliff dwellings and the Pueblo culture. Still others became the migratory tribes that followed the buffalo herds north and south on the Great Plains. And in the Midwest they became the Mound-Builders. In the South they were farmers. Along the Atlantic shore they were both farmers and fishermen. Those who finally came into New England, which was settled late by the Indians, were farmers first, fishermen second.

When I look at collections of arrow and spear points and other chipped stone tools made by those early New England Indians I nearly always think what poor artisans they were. Compared with similar tools and weapons made by the High Plains Indians, those found in New England are crude, definitely of inferior workmanship. Then I think of why these show less than artistic perfection. The New England Indians were essentially farmers. They didn't hunt the same way the Plains Indians did. They didn't need perfection in weapons. I suspect that if I could compare their hoes and their few other tools for working the soil with similar tools among the Plains Indians, there would be an equal contrast, this time in favor of New England's Indians.

In any case, these New England Indians were primarily farmers. They grew maize and tobacco, beans and squash. They grew more than they could use, stored the excess, sometimes traded it to other tribes. For meat, they took deer the easy way, usually in *drives* or *surrounds*. Sometimes they drove a herd of deer into a lake or a river, slaughtered those they needed, and left the rest to save themselves or drown. Sometimes they circled an area with fire, trapped game in the circle, and killed what they needed, leaving the rest to die or be maimed. For venison, they preferred fat young does, took them in preference to tough old bucks. In times of plenty they took only the choice parts and left the rest of the carcass for scavengers. Contrary to common belief today, they were not really conservationists. But there was so much game and there were so few Indians, relatively, that it didn't matter.

Also there were fish in great plenty. New England's seacoast and even its rivers teemed with mackerel, herring, cod, sturgeon, and flounder. There were scallops, mussels, crabs, oysters, and lobsters in the shallow inshore waters. Lobsters weighing as much as fifteen pounds were not unusual. Cod three to five feet long, sturgeon six to nine feet long, were common.

Europeans didn't discover this area, even this continent, according to the best records we can find, until the tenth century A.D. Then the Vikings came and went several times. One group of them spent a winter here among the Skraellings, as they called the Indians. This expedition ended in troubles that made the whole project untenable. There was food aplenty here, as well as grapes for wine, fur and timber for the taking. But there was dissension among the Vikings and there was woman trouble. Apparently they hadn't yet learned that a few women in a large group of men are as dangerous as a bomb. These troubles, along with Indian hostility, sent the survivors back to Greenland. There seem to have been no more attempts at settlement until the fifteenth and sixteenth centuries.

Spain, France, and England all became eagerly ambitious about this new world in the century after Columbus landed in the West Indies. Explorers swarmed up and down the coast from Cuba to the mouth of the St. Lawrence. Eventually the Spanish established themselves in the Caribbean Islands, in Mexico and Peru, and up the Pacific coast as far as present-day Oregon. The French took over the Canadian shore and interior along the Great Lakes. The English made the most of the territory between Canada and Florida, with their major settlements in Virginia and New England.

The Spanish frankly said they were looking for treasure, primarily gold and precious gems. They found and took a great deal of loot, and they lost much of it in shipwrecks at sea. The French were looking for fish and furs, and they, too, got more of these treasures than they could use. The English were looking for anything that could turn a profit—lumber, fur, fish, grain, gold, sassafras root, spices—and for that mysterious, elusive Northwest Passage that would be a shortcut to the Orient.

The first description of the New England coast seems to be that of Giovanni de Verrazano, an Italian explorer sent out by King Francis I of France. In 1524 Verrazano came up the coast and first smelled, then saw, "beautiful fields" and plains "full of the largest forests, some thin, some dense, clothed with various sorts of trees, with as much beauty and delectable appearance as it would be possible to express." These trees, he said, "for a long distance exhale the sweetest odors."

This was something many explorers mentioned, the fragrance that reached them well offshore. One voyager of that time says it was "so strong a smell, as if we had been in the midst of some delicate garden abounding in all kinds of odoriferous flowers, by which we were assured that the land could not be farre distant." "We smelled the odor a hundred leagues," wrote Verrazano, "and farther when they burned the cedars and the wind blew from the land."

Some of the explorers and many of the subsequent settlers spoke of the fragrance of strawberries as they approached land. Wild strawberries grew from Maine to Florida, and the explorers as well as the colonists marveled at them. There were strawberries in England and on the continent, but apparently the wild ones here in America were bigger and more flavorful. They certainly received praise and attention.

We still have wild strawberries, even after all the years of abuse and neglect. I know two or three places where I can go in June and pick as many as a pint of them. But the berries are small, the plants are what I call puny. Twenty years ago we set aside one small corner of the garden and transplanted a dozen wild strawberries into it, hoping to coddle them into exceptional production. They grew well for a few years, but produced only small berries, and few of them. Then the plants languished and died. Nearby, tame strawberry plants throve and produced the big, moderately flavorful fruit our hybridizers have created for commercial growers, berries that ship well and keep well on the retailer's counter.

I can't recall ever smelling strawberries from any distance. Burning cedar, yes. In late autumn you can smell it all up and down our valley. We use it for kindling in our fireplaces. But the most pervasive odors are of new-cut hay in early June and corn pollen in August. I class both of them as fragrances, and I am sure I could recognize them offshore a mile or more.

Verrazano passed Block Island, which he thought was beautifully wooded. John Winthrop, a century later, said Block Island was "overgrown with brushwood of oak–no good timber in it." Verrazano went on to Rhode Island and anchored in Narragansett Bay. From there, he and his men went inland eighteen or twenty miles and found wide, fertile fields, "open and devoid of every impediment of trees, of such fertility that any seed in them would produce the best crops." Later travelers found that the Narragansett Indians were among the best farmers on the Atlantic seaboard. They had made wide clearings, not only for farming but to produce tender new growth for browse to attract deer.

New England at that time was almost entirely wooded, except for clearings the Indians had made and an occasional natural meadow along the seashore. The trees were part of the great pine and hardwood forest that covered much of the northern United States. There is a tradition that those woodlands were so dense and uninterrupted that a squirrel could have traveled from the Atlantic shoreline to the Mississippi River without touching the ground. But this undoubtedly is an overstatement. All through that woodland, on testimony of later travelers, were clearings, both natural and man-made, some of them several miles in extent.

Among the earliest efforts at colonization by the English was the settlement on Monhegan Island, just off the coast of Maine, in 1606. The settlers there found little to encourage them to stay. Monhegan, after all, is essentially a big rock in a cold ocean. It served, and still does, as a center for cod and lobster fishermen, and the occupation gave England a territorial claim. But winter on Monhegan was miserable for those first settlers, and they didn't find summer much more to their liking. They packed up and went back to England in 1608.

Another early settlement was at Massachusetts Bay. Captain John Smith arrived there in 1614, after his notorious years in the Virginia colony, which culminated in the Pocahontas episode. From Massachusetts Bay, Smith launched a whale-fishing program to occupy the colony and make it profitable. There were plenty of whales, but the colonial fishermen didn't take even one. They abandoned whaling and Smith undertook to explore and map the coast, while others of the settlement began to trade with the Indians for furs and fish. Smith went up and down the coast in a small boat that needed only eight men to handle it. He went "from point to point, ile to ile, and Harbour to Harbour," trading, exploring, and mapping. "This Coast," he wrote, "is mountainous, and Iles of huge Rockes, but overgrowne for the most part with most sorts of excellent good woods." He was one of the few who ever praised New England's climate. He was impressed by the fisheries. New England cod and hake were, he said, two and three times as big as those from Canadian waters. Salmon were easy to catch as they ran up the rivers in the spring. Eels came up the rivers from the sea. Alewives by the million came up the rivers to spawn in the spring, and the settlers caught them by the barrelful. There were so many shellfish, the Indians couldn't make a dent in the supply. The settlers ate all they could and then let their hogs out on the beaches to root for clams and mussels.

When another group of English colonists nearly starved a few years later, Captain Smith snorted with scorn. He clearly thought these people were hare-brained religious cranks who didn't even try to adapt to wilderness life. But the early colonists and even some of the explorers were suspicious of America's native food. De Soto took a drove of hogs with him for meat, though he went through an area swarming with deer. French explorers in the Great Lakes area were at first reluctant to eat buffalo, though it was a basic item in the Indians' diet. These English colonists had lived a tamed life and had eaten only food from cultivated fields. They were not equipped temperamentally to live off the land.

Captain Smith saved a good many lives, nevertheless, by bartering with the Indians for corn, squash, beans, and venison. The hungry colonists ate, whether they liked the food or not, and eventually they learned to plant and grow their own supplies of this food.

The early New England settlements were all much alike. They sat on harbors, where ships could land easily. They arose either on the sites of previous Indian villages or in natural clearings. They were surrounded by woodland that soon was pushed back as trees were cut for fuel, for building material, to clear farmland, or simply to eliminate cover for hostile Indians or wild beasts. Whatever the reason, the woodland, much of it climax forest of huge old trees, was cut. The "densely wooded" shoreline and the nearby interior were stripped of their woodland within a relatively few years.

As more and more settlers arrived from England, the original communities became so crowded that new settlements began to split off. Most of them went inland, and the first areas occupied were those with the most fertile soil and those easiest to reach from the original settlements. By 1700, there were eighty thousand people in the area along the coast and up the great central valley of Connecticut and Massachusetts as far as Northfield. After that, the tide of settlement pushed westward and northward, out of the broad lowlands and into the more rugged area of stony hills. Here, in my end of Connecticut, Litchfield was founded in 1719. The immediate area where I live was nominally settled, by the English at least, in 1739.

And here is one of the amusing quirks of human history. The English reports say the first settlers came here from earlier settlements in the Connecticut valley or along the coast. But when I dig into reports from other than English sources I find that these "first settlers" found Dutch settlers already living here, farming and trading with the Indians. But they were Dutch, from settlements over along the Hudson. And this is the English who are telling this story. So "the first white settlement" here had to be English.

16

17

18

CHAPTER 3

To me, New England means trees, woodland. There are trees, magnificent forests, in my native West—in the Rockies, for example. The West Coast woodlands are incomparable, with their giants. The upper Midwest once was all woodland, and so was much of the Southeast. But they are not the same as New England somehow, not trees and people. New England is old elms on the village green. It is tree-lined country lanes. It is chestnuts littering the ground with prickly-husked nuts in the autumn, sugar maples producing sap by the bucketful in spring for syrup and sugar. Pines to make masts for the King's Navee, pines to cover the farmers' barns, pines to sheathe those beautiful eighteenth-century houses. It is hemlock for boards and planks, cedar for durable fence posts, and oak for any really tough job ever assigned to wood.

Trees.

And only after a moment do I remember that the elms have been dying for thirty years, of Dutch Elm Disease. That the chestnut blight has wiped out virtually every chestnut tree in New England, leaving only such reminders as persistent sprouts in the backwoods that spring from old stumps, thrive for a few years, then are stricken and die like all the sprouts before them. Or as the interior trim of this farmhouse where we live, which is of chestnut cut on this farm before the blight appeared. We forget the various enemies of pine and oak and hemlock. But this still is a land of trees, isn't it? Only the forester or the lumberman is choosy. We still have birches, don't we? And ash trees. We still have pasture cedars. What do you want? Black walnut and bird's eye maple? . . .

Of all the New England states, Maine is the most heavily wooded. It is today, and it was when the first white men came. When we go to Maine, we go to lumbermen's country. And to a land of resort lakes, of summer camps, of rocky coast, rugged islands, lobster fishermen, potato farms. The potato farms are the only really sizeable gaps in the Maine woods. Only 25 percent of Maine ever was cleared of its woodland. That was back in 1880. A good deal of tree growth has been renewed since then as farms were abandoned. A few years of abandonment brings back the trees.

Approximately three quarters of New England is now covered with woodland, and the remaining 25 percent includes all the cities and their sprawl of suburbs and villages. Typical of what happened over the decades is the story of Connecticut. It was settled early, and the woodland was cut over several times. By 1860, all but 27 percent of the state was open land, its trees all cut. But by 1910, abandonment of hillside farms had left so many fields open for second-growth timber that almost twice as much land was forested, some 45 percent of the state. This trend continued, and by 1955 the trees had taken over 63 percent of the total area of Connecticut. The total today must be close to 75 percent.

Two examples indicate what happened, not only here but elsewhere. Just across the river from our farm is a tract of second-growth timber that looks as though it has been growing there untouched for 100 years. Such land is called *sproutland* on the local tax rolls. It is a tangle of trees, vines, and underbrush that only rabbits and grouse love; few people go there because it is such a maze. A few years ago a crewman for the power company told me that when he was a small boy, close to fifty years ago, the whole tract was a cow pasture—grass with a few old pines for shade. Then the land was sold, the pasture was abandoned, and the trees began to come back.

Just beyond the mountain back of our house is one of the small glacial lakes of this area. Its shores are lined with summer cottages set in a generous fringe of white pines and red cedars. The owner of one of the larger shoreline areas, which he inherited from his father, told me that when he was a boy the whole lakeshore was open grassland, much of it used as hay fields for adjoining farms. Then much of the hay land was sold to people who built cottages and docks and didn't mow the seedlings that sprang up. Seedlings became trees, cottagers like their shade, and today it is a tree-wreathed lake.

The first extensive tree cutting in this area, as elsewhere in New England, was done by white settlers to clear fields for farming. The Indians had cleared land for fields, but never more than a few acres at a time. Their stone hand-axes were not the tools needed to fell a tree two feet or more in diameter. They could girdle it and let it die, then weaken it with fire and wait for a storm to bring it down. But the early settlers brought iron axes and saws. They cut the trees, let them dry, then burned them. Or they split beams from the logs for their houses. But they didn't cut trees to build log cabins. The log cabin was unknown in America until the Swedes set up a colony in Delaware in 1638. It was a Swedish invention and it spread slowly in America. New England never really was a log-cabin colony.

When the plowable land had been cleared and fields developed, the settlers turned to the rocky hillsides and began cutting trees to open what would become pastureland. With the trees cut, the grass soon grew and the farmers had grazing areas for cattle and sheep. Over the years, probably more land was cleared for pastures than for fields.

Then, here in this area, high-grade iron ore was discovered in 1732. That changed the whole picture.

Iron-making was not new in America. The colonists knew the technique used in Europe for centuries, and they used it to make nails, horseshoes, muskets, farm tools, and other ironware they needed. They even exported iron to England, which was short of trees to make charcoal, an essential in the iron-making process of that day. By 1648, John Winthrop Jr., son of the Massachusetts governor, had two blast furnaces going near Boston. In 1648, he built another just east of New Haven. Other people built several furnaces in Massachusetts and Connecticut. All of the furnaces had to use poor quality ore, usually "bog iron" dredged from nearby ponds.

Then Salisbury iron was discovered in the 1730s. It was of high quality and there was plenty of it. There was plenty of limestone, too, almost anywhere you chose to open a quarry. All the hills were wooded, providing the raw material for charcoal. Everything needed for the iron industry was here, except roads. Transport as well as travel still was largely limited to horse and pack saddle. The iron was not exploited until 1762, when a blast furnace was built at what now is Lakeville. Ethan Allen was one of three partners at that furnace, but restless Ethan didn't stay long. He took a major part in another furnace at Canaan, Connecticut, and from there went to Vermont. The Lakeville furnace worked overtime during the Revolution, making iron cannons, grenades, mortars, and camp kettles for the colonial army. Another major furnace eventually was established on nearby Mount Riga, and it continued to produce high-quality iron until about 1908.

And that is a long way of saying that the trees in this area were cut for charcoal for the local iron industry. Most of the hills still have marks of those old charcoal "pits," as they are called, where the wood was piled in beehive structures and fired with smouldering flame that had to be tended day and night. Many of the hills were stripped of trees for charcoal. Eventually the iron industry moved to Pittsburgh and the local trees had a chance to grow again. The next time they were cut it was for lumber and for conversion into pulp to feed the paper mills. You can find small sawmills scattered through the western Massachusetts and Connecticut hills today, turning out native white pine boards and dimension lumber, occasionally sawing a wild black cherry log with special care, or a length of special rock maple.

The sawyers in these little mills, at least those whom I have known, are friendly men who love wood. One man, who now is retired, always had a special treasure to show me when I stopped at his mill—a beautifully patterned rock maple board, a perfect piece of white oak, a slab of pasture cedar red as a winesap. Knowing I had a lathe and occasionally turned a bowl or a salad plate, he saved unusual odds and ends for me. And when I needed lumber, he always had good advice as well as good lumber, properly sawed and seasoned.

Somewhere long ago, in an old, forgotten book, I read that "seasoning" saw logs doesn't really mean letting them dry. At least, it didn't in the old days. It meant cutting the logs at the right season of the year. The season was governed by the moon as well as the month: Timbers cut during "the old moon in January," or under the right conditions in February, "will stand straight and true," the old rule said; if you cut your logs "when the moon is full, timber fibers warp and pull."

I asked my sawyer friend about this, and he smiled and said, "The old-timers cut some pretty good lumber." And he would say no more. But I know that the lumber I got from him has stood straight and true, barn doors as well as indoor paneling. And I know that the fine old barns, the really old ones, and the beautiful old houses indicate that the men who built them knew what they were doing. The lumber in them nearly always is straight and true, even after all these years. How much the moon's phases had to do with it can only be guessed, but there's no denying that the wood was seasoned to perfection. Maybe farmers always cut sawlogs in January and February because that was a slack time and because there was snow on which to skid the logs out of the woods.

There always has been a certain amount of tree-cutting for fuel. The fireplace may be an inefficient means of heating a house, but for a long time it was the best one available. And there was no shortage of wood to burn. Then New Englanders advanced from the fireplace to the enclosed stove to the furnace, substituting coal for wood, then oil for coal, and eventually gas and electricity for oil in many places. But the fireplace persists. The open fire has a special beauty for many of us, whether it is economical or not. I was amused when I first saw an ultra-modern house built by an ultra-modern architect for himself, with all the outside walls made of glass and with a fireplace in the central chimney. It seemed a little like equipping a rocket to the moon with a dashboard and a whip-socket.

I came late to the fireplace and the open hearth, so I had to learn about firewood instead of knowing about it almost by instinct. Natives, at least New England countrymen, seem to know all about these things from the time they can tote a stick of firewood. Even so, I am constantly amazed at what so many people, guests as well as hired help, don't know about fire and fireplaces.

Ashes, first of all. When we have a new helper in the house, I always have to issue orders and stand guard over the ashes in the Franklin stove. Helpers seem to think any hearth with ashes is messy and must be cleaned. Any experienced fire-maker knows that without ashes, nobody can build a good fire or keep one going. You need ashes to help direct the draft, to hold the heat under the logs, to control a too-eager flame. Properly used, ashes can hold a fire overnight, so all you need do in the morning is add a bit of kindling and a dry stick or two to get the fire going again. Ashes are priceless. But household help and even some wives have no respect for them. The fire-maker must be firm about this.

Then there is the matter of building a fire. You don't just pile up the wood and light a match. You *build* a fire, literally build it, with a large, slow-burning log at the back, a smaller log in front, kindling and split, dry wood between. There should be a small pocket in the ashes under the kindling, just big enough to take a wadded-up half-page of newspaper. Be sure the damper is open, and if there is any doubt about the draft, light a small twist of paper and hold it in the fireplace's throat, where it can start a warm draft up the chimney. Then light the paper under the kindling, and you should be in business.

Choosing the firewood is another essential, really the first on the list. Unless you have your own woodlot, this may be difficult. Even here in my area some of the "cordwood" advertised for sale is really bonfire wood, anything that came to hand while the woodcutter was at work. Perhaps the most worthless wood is sawmill waste, most of it native pine bark-slabs cut to fireplace length. It burns like paper and with just about as much heat.

I have seen several lists of "best" firewoods. They all differ somewhat. I have my own list, and it doesn't follow any of them all the way. For a back log, I prefer oak or hickory. For a front log, I like either oak or maple or, if it is available, apple. Any fruit wood has a special fragrance. Maple, especially hard maple, makes excellent fireplace wood if properly seasoned; it even makes a good back log if not too dry. A few years ago we had to cut one of our big sugar maples, which was badly rotted and would have taken down the whole power line if it had fallen. We took it down, cut it to fireplace size, and piled it in a rick near the woodshed. When I looked at it a year later, that maple had rotted so badly it wasn't worth burning. It's still there for squirrels and chipmunks to play tag in. That taught me how vulnerable even hard maple is to the weather.

Ash is excellent firewood with a clean, sweet smell. It is one of the few woods that burn well while still green; its sap, I am told, is inflammable. Some years ago an old-line New Englander quoted an old saying to me: "Ash green is fit for a queen." The only other wood I know that burns well while green is gray birch, the despised weed tree that most New Englanders won't bother to bring in the house. Cut and left on the ground, gray birch rots in a few months. Dead and still standing, however, it makes good kindling. White birch, the old-time canoe-birch, makes a good fire but is too rare around here to use for fuel. Black birch is good firewood and has a pleasant odor, something like fruit wood.

Elm never was much good as fireplace wood. Some elm burned with a urine smell and was colloquially known as "piss-elm." Dead, it has no value except as kindling. Chestnut was full of explosive sparks. But even dead chestnut now is hard to find and most of it is punky.

Poplar, aspen, cottonwood—often the names are used interchangeably—makes good kindling and a quick, hot fire, but has no lasting quality. Pine and cedar make excellent kindling, but tamarack tops them all with its resiny wood. However, tamarack, sometimes called *larch,* leaves lots of soot in the chimney and creates a chimney fire hazard.

Go down the list. Any hickory makes good fireplace wood. Walnut and butternut also are excellent, but too valuable for furniture and other special uses to be used as fuel. Sycamore is definitely inferior. Chokecherry makes good firewood, with a fruity fragrance.

The charcoal era in this area ended about 1885, and the extensive tree-cutting did too. The woods began to come back on all the hills that had been stripped. But when you cut a virgin forest it doesn't just grow back the way it was, if you leave it alone for a few years. It takes time, a long time—about two hundred years, some say—and the growth goes through several stages.

First new growth on clear-cut woodland soil are the fast-growing trees that need lots of sunlight. And of course those that produce lots of seeds that are easily distributed, by the wind or by the birds. Gray birch and white pine are among the very first, the birch because it is hardy and persistent, the pine because it grows fast and thrives in grassy places. That is why old pastures so often grow up as groves of white pine—there usually is an old pine or two left for shade in the pasture, and the seedlings spread and take over.

After the birch and pine come red maples and other second-rate trees that can tolerate shade. Eventually they are joined by—or displaced by—sugar maple, beech, ash, oak, and hemlock, all trees that will persist in moderate shade. The birch and pine age and die. Then the red maples go. That leaves the sugar maple, beech, ash, and oak dominating, with the hemlock always there in the background. And eventually it is the hemlock that persists. Few other trees have the persistence of hemlock here in this area. Once it is established, it can withstand almost anything except fire.

Here in southern New England, it is the red cedars, or pasture cedars as they are often called, that creep into neglected pastures first. They are planted in bird droppings and often are found along pasture fences, even when the pastures are still in use and cared for. The pastures on our farm are divided into several lots by barbed wire fences, and all these division fences have a few cedars growing along them. One fence near a small grove of cedars has as fine a row of fifteen-foot cedars as one might ask, at least ten of them in a perfect line with the fence posts and about twenty feet apart. They probably would scatter out over the pasture, too, if we didn't mow it at least once every summer to keep down the seedlings and rank grass. But we never mow the fence line.

Since the turn of the century, most of the good pine has been cut in central and southern New England. What has been left, generally speaking, is what foresters and lumbermen call "trash." But the newcomers to the land, most of them outlanders even if from New England's own cities, cherish their trees. Few of them want their woodland to be "harvested" or even to be selectively thinned. Perhaps it would be better woodland if it were thinned, but they like it the way it is. As one man said to me, "I don't want my place to be a park. I want it natural, the way it would grow if everybody would keep his hot hands off." And no matter what the professional forester says, that is the way it is going to be.

Come to think of it, that's the way I reacted a few years ago when a stranger came to the door and said he wanted to buy a few trees. What he meant by "a few trees" was the birch-ash-maple tangle on about twenty acres of the mountainside. It is an old field grown up naturally, and this man was buying pulp wood for one of the paper mills up the river in Massachusetts. I said no, the trees were not for sale. He gave me his sales talk: It was waste land the way it was; the trees were of no value as trees; if they were taken off, the really good trees would have a chance to grow there. And he would pay so much an acre. More than enough to pay taxes on that land.

I still said no. Those trees didn't offend my eyes and they weren't hurting the land. Eventually they will give way to better trees, just in the natural course of growth. Meanwhile, taxes on that land were not really burdensome.

The man went away shaking his head in bewilderment. It didn't make sense to him. His whole approach to life was shaped by the dollar. My only objection to that is his inability to understand my approach, which is somewhat different. I respect the dollar myself, but even more I respect life, all kinds of life, green and leafy as well as red and blood-nourished, and I want more time, more room, more opportunity to try to learn its meaning. Even under the best of circumstances, that area of weed trees which the man wanted to cut and make into paper pulp cannot produce really big, mature trees during my own lifetime. But it can evolve from cut-over brush land toward natural woodland, and perhaps I can learn a few things by living with it the rest of my life.

I suspect that there are quite a few others who feel the same way about their woods, and by no means all of them have my sense of awe at the very sight of a tree. I grew up, after all, in a land where there were virtually no trees. A great many of the "rural nonfarm" people, as they are called by census takers, are New Englanders who grew up with trees but who never owned one until they retired to twenty acres of old pastureland with a farmhouse and three gnarled apple trees in the dooryard. They, too, think of the woodland as something special, something as enduring as these rocky New England hills.

21

22

23

25

26

CHAPTER 4

IN WRITING ABOUT NEW ENGLAND, one is tempted to make broad, flat statements because it is a relatively small area tucked quite neatly into a compact corner of the nation. But of all the distinct regions in the United States, New England is probably the least uniform, in geography, in climate, in ethnic origins, in interests and occupations, and in natural resources.

But let's risk a generalization and say that geographically there are three major areas. One, the earliest known to European explorers and the first settled, is the coastal region. The next consists of the interior valleys, New England's major agricultural area until industry began displacing the farmer and now, particularly in Connecticut and Massachusetts, the industrial heart of the area. The third district is the hill country of the north and west—western Connecticut and Massachusetts and much of New Hampshire and Vermont. Maine is a kind of law unto itself, but it also has three distinct areas: the coast, the major interior valleys, and the timber-and-lakes country to the north and west.

For a long time, the coastal people, particularly of Massachusetts, looked down their noses at the inlanders. Some of them still do. Their forebears were the original settlers. They established Puritanism in America. Out of their church rule came civil government and a system of education. Traditions they fostered were to a large degree responsible for the Revolution, which ended English rule and forced the colonies to establish a new form of government.

Education and books have a particular interest for me, and not merely because I have been a word man all my life. Books are the accumulated knowledge and wisdom of the human race, and I believe we owe it to ourselves and those around us to share in this legacy which makes man more than a two-legged animal with the unique ability to communicate in more than squeals and grunts.

The early colonists were self-righteous and domineering in a way, but they did inaugurate popular education. True, the early schools were opened for religious purposes. The colonists believed in preachers who could understand the Bible and worshipers who could understand what the preachers were talking about in their interminable sermons. In 1636, the General Court of the Massachusetts Bay Colony appropriated money to start the College of Newtowne or Cambridge, which was to train preachers and laymen in the fundamentals of Godly thinking and living. The college was then endowed by John Harvard with his books and his money, and it took his name. Popular education in the colony dates from 1647, when a law was enacted requiring that every town of fifty families establish and maintain an elementary school, and that towns twice that size and larger have secondary schools. These were not free schools, but they were open to all who wanted to attend and had the tuition.

Connecticut established the first free public schools in New Haven in 1642 and in Hartford in 1643. By 1650, Connecticut had enacted schooling laws much like those of Massachusetts. Penalties were imposed on parents who failed to educate their children and the towns were given the right to take boys from homes where they were not being properly schooled and to apprentice them to masters who would educate them and teach them useful trades.

Connecticut began educating Indians and Negroes at an early date, relatively speaking. In 1735, an institution called Moor's Indian Charity School was started at Columbia, near present-day Willimantic, by the Reverend Eleazor Wheelock. There Indian students were taught the English language and the fundamentals of Christian religion, training designed to equip them to become missionaries to their own people. The school was supported in good part by contributions from well-known men both here and abroad, including Lord Dartmouth in England and King George II. It continued with moderate success until 1769, when enrollment had dropped to such a low point that the school was moved to Hanover, New Hampshire, "to increase its usefulness." Whites as well as Indians were admitted, and it became Dartmouth College.

Negro schooling didn't come until the 1800s, but even then it was a daring venture and roused what might be termed a foretaste of the 1970s in Boston. Miss Prudence Crandall, a Quaker, had established a school for girls in Canterbury, not far from the original site of the Indian school. All went well until 1832, when she accepted a Negro girl as a pupil. There was an immediate revolt. All the other pupils walked out and didn't come back. Miss Crandall capped that reaction by turning her school into an institution exclusively for "young ladies and little misses of color." That really roused the animals. Feeling ran so high that the Connecticut legislature was besieged, and it rammed through the "Black Law" that made it illegal to establish a school for Negroes without permission of the local authorities.

This happened less than thirty years before the Civil War. Already there was quite a bit of traffic on the "Underground Railroad," a secret organization of antislavery sympathizers that conducted escaped slaves northward to freedom in Canada. A good deal of this traffic came through Connecticut. One of the "main lines" was up here, through western Connecticut. Friends of ours have shown us the dark and musty basement hideaway in their handsome family house, where slaves on their secret way north were hidden until word came that it was safe to pass them along to the next station.

John Brown, of Harper's Ferry fame and well remembered out where I came from for the bloody midnight raids he and his border-ruffian sons led in Kansas, was born only twenty miles or so from where we live. The house is on a back road near Torrington, Connecticut. But local people aren't particularly proud of mad old John. A very modest sign marks the lane leading to the house, and there are no local legends about him, as there are, for instance, about Ethan Allen.

But I was talking about books and education, not the Civil War.

I have no figures on the number of preparatory schools in New England, but I am sure there are well over 100. Three well-known schools, Hotchkiss, Salisbury, and Berkshire, are within ten miles of our farm. Almost every year, a lad from one of them arrives at our door, lost and frightened. He has flunked a course, been reprimanded, can no longer play hockey or soccer, is in disgrace, and has wandered off and can't find his way back. May he use our telephone to call his father, or somebody? We take him in, assure him that he really isn't lost, listen to him for half an hour as he unloads his juvenile troubles, tell him he will recover and live and even play hockey again. And I dream up a reason for going past his school on an errand, take him along, and we never hear from him again. Today's young seem never to have learned to say "thank you."

Add to these preparatory schools almost one hundred colleges, and New England has what must be called a thriving education business. The colleges and universities are among the most prestigious in America and, for that matter, the world. And

New Englanders are a literate people, with an unusually high percentage of them college educated.

But literacy has been a mark of the New Englander from early colonial days. Books were precious. As I mentioned earlier, John Harvard's books and money got a college named for him. Others also gave money, but his books were rare and made John Harvard's gift memorable.

My home town of Salisbury organized one of the first library associations in the country in 1771, only thirty-two years after the township was settled. And in 1803 it established the first tax-supported library in the United States. That library, the Scoville Library, is still very much in business, with an excellent collection of books and a high percentage of the townspeople as patrons.

That is typical of New England. There are public libraries in every town. Massachusetts boasts more public libraries than any other state except New York, which is almost five time as big as Massachusetts. But Massachusetts has more library volumes per capita than even New York. There is a bit of a let-down, however, if one follows the statistics a little further. Ohio, for instance, with one-third fewer library books than Massachusetts, has more library readers. There may be consolation in the fact that Ohio was settled largely by people of New England stock.

Now and then I am asked why New England has produced so many writers. There is one rather obvious answer. The number of writers per capita is not phenomenally high, particularly if you limit the per capita count to literate people. But certain facts do persist. The early colonists were dissenters and, if I may say so, a garrulous lot. Their preachers preached sermons that lasted hours, and the laymen argued endlessly about the Scriptures and their interpretation. The tradition has come down that New Englanders are laconic, and some of them are. But others can out-talk anyone I ever met in the Midwest or the South. After New England outgrew its intense religious beginnings, some of that verbal energy went into folk tales and extended fables in the form of fiction. For example, Melville's *Moby Dick* and almost all of Hawthorne's stories. Fables, they were, morality tales.

Another reason for New England's unusual number of writers is proximity to market. New York and Boston for many years have been the publishing centers for the United States. Writers want to sell their product to magazine editors and book publishers, and it seems easier if they live close to their market. This has prompted a persistent migration into lower New England, especially into Connecticut, by writers who want access to New York or Boston but don't want to be trapped in artists' enclaves where talk too often substitutes for work.

The records show, however, that publishing started early in New England. Stephen Day launched a press in Cambridge in 1638. There were a few other presses in the seventeenth century, but most of them were brief ventures. Soon after the Revolution, in 1778, Alden Spooner started a press in New Hampshire. In 1780, Judah Spooner and Timothy Greene started a press in Vermont. One was started in Maine in 1785 by Benjamin Titcomb and Thomas Wait. Today New England has more than thirty small publishers besides the two big ones in Boston—Houghton Mifflin and Little, Brown and their subsidiaries.

The Bread Loaf Summer School of English, conducted by Middlebury College in Vermont since the 1920s, has encouraged writers, and the Writers' Conference at Bread Loaf set the pattern for similar conferences all over the country. For many years, Robert Frost participated in the Bread Loaf Conference. (Frost, by the way, though one of New England's and America's great poets, was not a native Yankee. He was born in San Francisco and didn't come to New England until he was ten years old. The family, however, did have New England roots.)

Middlebury's summer school pattern was followed by other arts. Yale had a Summer Music School at Norfolk, Connecticut, with concerts and distinguished composers. The Tanglewood Summer Concerts at West Stockbridge, Massachusetts, have become one of the country's major musical events. Internationally known composers, musicians, and conductors appear there, with the Boston Symphony Orchestra at the heart of the program. Not far away, at Jacob's Pillow, is the Summer Dance Group's colony and theatre, founded by Ted Shawn and Ruth St. Denis. For many years the group has presented world-famous programs.

All over New England one finds summer theatre, in every kind of playhouse, from an old barn to a beautiful, modern theatre such as the one at Stratford, Connecticut. The summer theatres have provided tryouts for any number of new plays as well as for countless aspiring actors and actresses, and for the past twenty years the more soundly based theaters have staged distinguished revivals of the better plays on Broadway. New England's summer theatre has been hailed as the best to be found anywhere in this country, and there seems no reason to dispute that claim. Summer music, dance, and theatre have become major assets of this corner of the country.

Now and then someone asks why New England has produced so many nature writers. The answer is complex, though it begins with the fact that the early settlers were surrounded by nature. That was true of early colonists everywhere, of course. But nature was, and still is, insistent here. Spring comes with a tremendous outburst of green leaves, sweet flowers, and birdsong. Summer is hot and wet and bursting with growth. Fall is unbelievably beautiful, such a display of leaf color and autumn flowers as the newcomers had never before seen. Winter is cold and snowy, but has its own frigid beauty.

New Englanders from the first were aware of nature. But they seldom wrote about it for others to read, except in letters and journals. Those who wrote for publication copied English writers and rhapsodized about the beauties of raw nature and the joys of hardship. They were parlor poets using what they believed was literary language. To get at the deeper feelings and honest emotions of the early colonists, one must go to the old journals and diaries. There one finds comments such as these:

> February is a miserable time. I would gladly pass it by . . . Now comes the deepest snow. Now we get the remainderment of winter . . . Jno's fingers were badly bitten by frost today and my knees ache from the cold . . . I yearn for March, inclement as it usually is. And April, though it means field work again.

Eventually Henry Thoreau wrote and published his observations and comments, and though his books were largely ignored at the time, they did set a new tone for writing about nature. For Thoreau, nature was insistent. For those who followed him, it still is. And the writer being in a sense an opportunist, writing about things at hand, inevitably there would be nature writers. Certainly more nature writers than those who wrote treatises on the obscurities of the Scriptures.

I spoke earlier of the three major areas of New England, and I have been writing primarily about the coastal region. Now a look at the interior valleys.

Those interior valleys were settled early primarily because they were easy to reach. One simply went up the river, usually by boat. Few of New England's major rivers have important barriers to boat traffic in their lower reaches. So settlements were established in the interior valleys simply because better farmland was available there than along the seacoast. Some communities were set up by speculators, of course, who bought and sold land to make a profit. At least one inland settlement was established in answer to a request from the local Indians, who believed a white settlement would discourage raids on their own communities by rival Indians.

These inland communities generally followed the English pattern of the day: the dwellings grouped in a village surrounded by the farmland. Nobody actually dwelt on the farms. This arrangement provided the comforts and friendship that the settlers needed, not to speak of relative safety from hostile Indians. Even so, life was centered in the home. Women's lives were filled with domestic tasks—everything from cooking to weaving and candle-making. The men used long winter evenings to make such tools as wooden pitchforks, axe handles, and ox-yokes; they spent hours mending harness and other equipment and making bowls, porringers, and pails for household use. They used their hands in a score of useful tasks. And when, a generation or two later, the first small industries were started on the waterways, using water wheels to power their simple machines, there were plenty of adept hands and clever minds to run those machines.

Thus were New England's first factories established. And as soon as the local markets were supplied, some of the manufacturers sent out agents or went out themselves to sell their wares. They were the first Yankee peddlers. They went afoot, carrying packs of notions, buttons, pins, combs, brass kettles, clocks, and tinware; and they traveled as far west as the Mississippi River and as far south as New Orleans. Some peddlers from Connecticut also sold fake nutmegs, carved of wood by local cheats, which didn't endear the peddlers to their customers and pinned the ironic title, Nutmeg State, on Connecticut. But most of the wares sold by these itinerants were first-rate. And Connecticut clocks became a standard against which clocks made elsewhere were judged.

Most of the industries began as household work. The textile industry, which became New Hampshire's foremost factory work, was a family matter until early in the eighteenth century. Almost every household had its flock of sheep and field of flax, and the loom was as commonplace as the trestle-table. The manufacture of boots and shoes was at first done by itinerant cobblers who went from cabin to cabin making crude footwear from leather the settlers had tanned for themselves. Then "cobblers' towns" appeared, where everyone had a hand in shoemaking. From there, it was a short and logical step to shoe factories.

In Connecticut, the early industries centered around brass, with clocks a foremost item. The first clocks had hand-carved wooden gears, but Yankee ingenuity eventually made those gears from brass, then found ways to make them interchangeable. That was the beginning of machine manufacture of intricate parts. The new method led to mass production of firearms and was the groundwork for today's automobile production lines.

So, out of those long winter evenings when the inland farmers developed manual skills and pondered new ideas about machines came today's industrial dominance through central New England.

The third New England area, the hill country to the north and west, has still another story. I can tell it best in terms of my own region, which is more or less typical.

As the seacoast and interior valleys were settled, the Indians were pushed back into the western hills. The Pequots, who dominated what now is eastern Connecticut, resisted until 1636. In that year, forces from Boston, Hartford, Wethersfield, and Windsor, with the help of the Mohicans, made a concerted attack and killed or captured virtually all the Pequots. Those who survived were sold as slaves to colonists in Bermuda—one of the first slavery deals made by New Englanders. After that, there was relative peace. The Mohicans had been decimated by disease before the whites arrived and were quite willing to sell or barter their claims to the land.

The Indians did not think in terms of land ownership. To them, nobody could own the land, not in the white man's sense. It was yours while you lived on it, but if you moved, it could belong to anyone who came to live on it. So the Indians took the money offered for "title" to the land and moved away. When they were told they could never come back, that was a different story. To add to the problem, the colonists looked on such deals as mere formalities anyway, saying they already had title to the land from the English King. Roger Williams was one of the few who dissented. In a letter to Governor Bradford he demanded, "Why lay such stress upon your patent from King James? 'Tis but parchment. James had no more right to give away or sell Massasoit's land and cut and carve his country than Massasoit would have to sell King James' Kingdom or to send Indians to colonize Warwickshire." Mr. Williams, you may recall, also had eccentric religious ideas and finally was told to go away and start his own colony. Which he did, in Rhode Island. And the leaders in Boston and Hartford continued to rely on the colonial patent from King James, which led to more and more resentment and eventually to King Philip's War. After that bloody and finally unsuccessful attempt to drive out the colonists, there was little Indian trouble, except from the French and Indian raids from Canada, down the wilderness corridor south from Champlain, down the Berkshire and Taconic Mountains.

Despite the threats of such raids, land speculators were busy in this "Western

Lands" area. They made deals with local Indians, applied to Hartford or Boston for confirmation of title, then sold the land in parcels to hardy settlers or other speculators. Straggling settlement, however, was discouraged, and in 1724 the General Assembly in Hartford put a no-trespassing sign on the land in the northwest corner of Connecticut, which was to await "further disposal of this Assembly." After surveys and reports, plans were finally announced in 1737 for "the sale and Settlement of all the Townships on the Western Lands." Seven townships were laid out, each divided into fifty-three rights or shares, fifty to be sold outright, the other three to provide income for the first settled minister, the church, and the schools.

The townships were not named then, but became Canaan, Cornwall, Goshen, Kent, Norfolk, Salisbury, and Sharon. By October, 1738, the auctions had been held for all towns, and all shares were sold at 150 to 200 pounds each. Settlement began almost at once. So did resale of shares, for a good many of the purchasers were land speculators. But within a few years the resident families had settled down and were raising big families, as well as hay and corn and cows and sheep.

By then the rigors of Puritan orthodoxy had begun to ease off, particularly outside the original centers of the church. Connecticut was a Puritan stronghold, but various "toleration acts" of the General Assembly amended the old restrictions. Church membership was simplified. Anglicans were not only tolerated, but their church was allowed "Church rates," or taxes, paid by their members. Quakers and Baptists were exempted from such taxes and allowed to participate in town meetings.

Even such eccentrics as Ethan Allen were tolerated. He wasn't an infidel, after all. He was an agnostic who happened to believe in reincarnation rather than in heaven. After the Revolution, contemporary writers reported that, "infidel opinion is coming in like a flood," and that quite a few young men "think of themselves as wiser than their fathers." Apparently an old, old complaint.

Meanwhile the farmers cleared the land and plowed and planted it. Most of the early farms were hillside and hilltop farms. Farmers built New England's miles and miles of stone walls with stones they took from their fields to make way for the plow, stones brought here by the glaciers. They may have built their houses on the hills because they believed the lowland "miasma" was unhealthful, but those upland fields were small and the soil shallow. It was good soil, what there was of it. The upland pastures were good, too, but so rocky that, as dry-witted Yankees said, New Englanders could raise only sharp-nosed sheep that could graze between the rocks.

Gradually, those hillside farms were worked out, their thin soil cropped to death or washed away. In the West, in the Ohio country and beyond, there was new land, level land with few rocks. Land where new, economical, labor-saving machinery could be used. Canals and lake shipping and railroads were providing low-cost transportation for western grain to eastern markets. After the Civil War the young generation was full of restlessness as well as ambition. Industry was expanding swiftly all through the central areas, and in the hills the old farm economy was becoming outmoded.

In the next few years, farms were abandoned by the score. The trees grew on the hills again. New England's rural history was being written on the land itself.

28

29

32

33

CHAPTER 5

IN THE BEGINNING, when the Europeans first settled here, New England had its full share of bird and animal life. It even had woods bison and moose and elk down here in Connecticut. Moose, for that matter, were still found on Long Island in the early eighteenth century. Those big game animals soon disappeared, not liking human company. But other animal life persisted, and a good deal of it still does.

Not long ago I read the observation of one man that the animals in this country now are all "tamed," that they are afraid of woods and the wilderness and want to spend their lives in contact with man. That, of course, is a fatuous observation made by a person who can't see more than two blocks beyond his subway station or bus stop. It probably reflects his own fear of the open country. There certainly are "dependent" animals—rats, mice, many squirrels, some raccoons, and some skunks—and they are the ones most often seen in the suburban areas. There are even white-tailed deer that haunt the pastures and field crops of nearby farms. And every summer camp has its population of mendicant coons and squirrels. But for every beggar that depends on man for a living there are hundreds, even thousands, that neither need nor want such charity.

New England, being so populated and so near to the woods and open fields even in its cities and midland towns, does have its full share of "dependent" animals. But it also has the truly wild ones, even after all these years of settlement. And, because of climate changes, we also have several animals and birds that are so alien to the area that they are almost like visitors from another age.

The first year we lived here my dog chased some small animal away from his food dish one winter evening. I held my breath, hoping it wasn't a skunk. It wasn't. It was an opossum. I got a flashlight and cornered the little beast beside the woodshed. It was the prettiest possum I ever saw, in prime pelage, silvery gray body, white head, a very pink nose, and eyes that glowed like rubies in the light. It wasn't particularly afraid of me and apparently my dog knew and had a kind of truce with it. The dog went back to his food and I followed the possum around for half an hour, while it poked into our compost heap, tasted a shriveled windfall apple, looked in a grass clump for insect life. Finally it wandered down a cow path and across the pasture.

I see possums every winter here, and I have yet to see one that doesn't seem unhappy. They obviously don't like cold weather and snow. A couple of years ago when I had to go to the village before the snowplow had been through, I had to stop, both going and coming, to let a shivering possum climb out of the wheel tracks. On the way home I got out and herded the miserable little beast out of the roadway and into a clump of cedars where it at least had shelter. It obviously hadn't enough sense to take care of itself.

The opossum is North America's only marsupial, distant kin of the kangaroo. It migrated to this continent from South America during the Ice Age. Until fifty or sixty years ago, opossums never came north of Virginia. Then minor changes in climate seem to have lured them north, and now they are relatively common throughout much of New England. They really aren't equipped for even our comparatively mild northern winter, either physically or mentally.

Some years ago a government biologist took approximate measurements of the brain-boxes in various animal skulls by filling them with beans, then counting the beans. His results made possible some interesting comparisons. They showed the opossum brain was equal to 21 beans, that of the porcupine 70, the raccoon 150, the red fox 189, the coyote 325. In other words, the raccoon has more than seven times the brain capacity the opossum has, the red fox nine times as much. Even the porcupine, which is a pretty stupid animal, has more than three times the brain capacity of the opossum.

Not only is the possum short of brains, but its nervous system apparently is subject to short-circuits. Some investigators say that when a possum plays dead in the presence of danger it isn't an act; that the animal faints and goes into a coma. But for that I cannot vouch.

Possums interest me because of their feet. For years I was told by those who should know that man became a superior creature because his opposed thumb enabled him to hold tools and a stylus or a pen to make a record of his ideas, if any. That opposed thumb seemed a critical matter. But the opossum also has the opposed thumb, and never learned to use its feet particularly well for even the simplest animal tasks. It can't even climb skillfully without using its prehensile tail. Actually, the raccoon, without the opposed thumb, is one of the most manually dexterous of all wild animals.

The opossum, as I said, came north when we began having somewhat warmer winters. But few other animals have paid as much attention to the climate as the birds have.

The eastern cardinal, for example, until less than fifty years ago was strictly a southern bird. Then, early in the 1930s, I began seeing an occasional cardinal in eastern Pennsylvania. A few years later they appeared in southern Connecticut. Now they are relatively common in Connecticut and Massachusetts. The Audubon Christmas bird counts for the past nine years have shown as many cardinals as tufted titmice or downy woodpeckers in this area. They come to our dooryard every winter and eat food kicked from the feeders by the smaller birds. Only occasionally do they come to the feeders. But they make April mornings bright with their imperious whistled calls, and they make January mornings dazzling with their brilliant color, particularly against the snow. One pair of cardinals usually nests in a tangle of wild grape vines on our garden fence.

Another southerner who has come north into our milder climate and now spends the winter here is the mockingbird. For some reason nobody can explain, mockers have been year-round residents on Martha's Vineyard and Nantucket at least since the 1920s, and they have nested at several places on Cape Cod as well as in Springfield, Massachusetts, and at Northampton, Northfield, Groton, Boston, Rockport, and other places in that area. Here in western Connecticut mockingbirds have been seen every year for at least the past ten years, and they always appear in the Audubon bird counts. Most years have shown only eight or ten, during that Christmas-season count, but in 1970 the count reached thirty-three and in 1974 it came to thirty-four. About five years ago, in a mild spell during the winter, a mocker appeared at our farm and was here every day for almost a month, on the side lawn, apparently looking for insects. It never came near the feeder or the suet. I have never heard one singing here, but there have been a number of verified reports of their nesting and hatching.

Still another southerner, the turkey vulture or buzzard, has extended its breeding range into western Connecticut and Massachusetts. Officially this began in 1931, but few people were aware of it until around 1948, when the big birds were first generally recognized. When we came here in 1952, we saw vultures every week or so, sailing in those great, high circles, looking for carcasses on which to feed. Now they are a common sight all summer. They are important in the big picture, as scavengers who help clean up the earth after winter has thinned the wild herds. Normally they migrate southward, as do most of the hawks, but occasionally one or two stay over the winter. Last winter I saw one in January; saw it several times, in fact. Vultures are not lovable or even likeable birds. They are ugly, they stink, they look and act like agents of death. But as I said, they are necessary. And I know no other eastern bird that can soar as they do on the hill country's updrafts.

For a long time I thought robins were evolving a special subspecies, a winter-hardy breed that never migrated. We always had a few winter robins that took shelter in the hemlocks and went to the bogs in the daytime to feed. Some of them came to our side yard, even in January and February, when the snow had thinned away. And when they were seen in the village they were hailed as heralds of an early spring and were called foolhardy to come north so soon.

Then I learned about Newfoundland or black-backed robins, a subspecies already in existence that summers in Newfoundland and Nova Scotia and often migrates only as far south as lower New England. They undoubtedly were my winter robins. They still are. And they still are mistaken by spring-hungry people for mis-timed migrants from the south predicting a very early spring. Our own robins don't come up from Georgia and Florida until the thirty-degree isotherm gets up this way and stays. Most of our spring migrants follow that same rule. Though a good many of them come later, none of them come sooner.

Over the years and decades, New England has lost a few species. The first of which we know was the great auk. The auks were flightless birds, big as geese. Their flesh was said to be very tasty, certainly so to hungry sailors who had lived for weeks on salt-meat. The auks on the islands off the mouth of the Saint Lawrence were taken by the boatload in the early days of exploration and were killed to the last bird in 1844. There also were great auks in Maine, possibly even farther down the New England coast, but they, too, were killed and eaten. They usually were called penguins by the early explorers.

Passenger pigeons were here in great numbers when the first white settlers came. The pigeons were a nuisance; they ate the settlers' crops. But they also were edible. So the new settlers killed them. Some pigeons persisted, though, and were seen in Massachusetts and the Connecticut Valley until about 1880.

The wild turkey once was a common resident of New England, but it was pretty well eliminated by a combination of lumbering and overshooting. By the 1850s and 1860s it was rare, and by 1874 it seemed to have vanished. Later, in 1929, and then in 1938, '39, and '40, wild turkeys from Virginia and Michigan stocks were released in Massachusetts. Other flocks have been released since, particularly in the mountain woodlands of western Massachusetts. Cold winters and natural predators are their worst enemies, but the thoughtless gunner is also a problem. Five or six years ago we saw three wild turkeys, two hens and a gobbler, at the far edge of our home pasture. Where they came from, I have no idea, but through the glasses they looked healthy and in first-class condition. They made their way slowly along the edge of the woodland, as though looking for a place to hide a nest. We hoped they would find the oak grove a little way up the mountain and settle in. They wandered into the woods and that was the last we saw of them that day.

A few days later a neighbor mowing the rank grass in our lower pasture came to the house and said, "There's something down there I think you ought to see." So I went and found a turkey, one of the hens we had seen. It was dead. One leg had been broken by a gunshot through the thigh, and that whole leg was green with gangrene. It was less than fifty yards from the road. It obviously had been shot by some passerby, one of those "Hey, it moves! Shoot it!" maniacs.

We haven't seen a wild turkey since.

There once were quail here, too. But they were shot off and replaced with western quail, which in turn were shot off. Local stocking has been done here and there since the 1940s, but none of the stock birds seem to match the original "large, heavy, and pale New England quail" spoken of in old accounts. Two years ago, Barbara and I were out for a walk up the road on a June afternoon when I heard a bob-white call. I couldn't believe it, but after the second call I answered with my own whistled approximation. It called back. I answered again. We turned back toward the house before it called again, but it continued to call, and I to answer, all the way home. We came into the house and a few minutes later I heard the call in the dooryard. Two answers, and it flew into the big apple tree just back of the dining porch. We had a good look at it, and I stopped answering. Ten minutes later it flew down the valley, a lone and obviously a very lonely quail. I never saw or heard it again.

The animals, as I said, seem to have paid less attention to the climate than the birds have. In most instances, the animals have had their problems with man and his works.

I mentioned elk and moose and bison. New England also had caribou. They persisted in northern New Hampshire until 1885, and in Maine until the turn of the present century.

Some reports indicate that white-tailed deer were scarce when the first white settlements were established here, but I am skeptical. Deer had been a staple in the Indian diet for generations. I suspect that the newcomers simply didn't know how to hunt deer. After all, they weren't woodsmen, and in England the crown owned all the deer and anyone who killed one could be hanged. If you read about the Thanksgiving party the Pilgrims held in the fall of 1620, you get a somewhat different picture than that of scarce deer. The Pilgrims invited Massasoit and his followers for the feast, and when the Indians arrived and saw how little food there was, they went out and in a few hours brought back the carcasses of five freshly butchered deer.

Deer did become more numerous as trees were cut and fields were planted. Within a few years they were considered pests by the colonists. But they never were in danger of extermination in New England, and probably there are more deer today than ever before. They sometimes become a nuisance now, too, but in Connecticut any land-owner is allowed, with a proper permit, to kill deer on his own land at any time if they damage crops. This, of course, is a good excuse for local farm folk to have venison in the freezer, and a good many of them do the year around.

Panthers lived in the New England woodland in the early days, though they never were really numerous. Call them panthers and you hear echoes of their screams and quake with fear. Call them cougars and they aren't half so menacing, somehow. Call them mountain lions and they are remote, still big, ferocious cats but native to the mountain West. Actually, panthers (or cougars or mountain lions) are the most timid of the big cats. They will run at the sight or smell of men. The documented instances of attacks on people can be counted on the fingers of one hand. But the animal got a reputation as a vicious killer long ago, probably because the early settlers confused panthers with African lions. They are skillful hunters, can and do kill deer and other game. But they were early destroyed in New England. Now and then, however, one is reported or rumored, there is a degree of excitement and the old tales of blood-thirsty panthers are dusted off and repeated. To my knowledge, however, not one panther has been killed in New England in the past fifty years, at least. A few years ago there was a panther report here in western Connecticut and nearby Massachusetts. And one morning Barbara saw an animal that looked like a big, tawny cat at the far side of our home pasture. I did not see it, and when I went there later that day I found nothing like a panther track.

Others of the cat family are rather common here. The Canada lynx is still found in upper New England, from Massachusetts northward. The bobcat, a somewhat smaller version of the bob-tailed cat, is native to the whole of New England—and virtually all of the United States, for that matter. We have a family of bobcats resident on our mountain. One of them gave my dog quite a going-over the first year we lived here. I see their tracks in the snow from time to time, and a couple of winters ago one came down to the house in the night and tore a window feeder for the birds from its moorings, apparently because I had put a piece of suet in the feeder. I see tracks every winter, but I have yet to see my first Connecticut bobcat in the flesh.

In early colonial days, New England had its share of wolves, and the old horror stories are still handed down about them, though we now know enough to discount them. The wolves certainly killed deer and domestic livestock, but it is doubtful they ever attacked Little Red Riding Hood or any of her family. One lone she-wolf on a killing spree, however, was said to have killed seventy-five sheep and goats on the farm of Israel Putnam in East Hartford, Connecticut. So the fate of the wolves was sealed. They were wiped out completely in New England and never came back.

The wolf's first cousin, the coyote, and his second cousin, the fox, have quite different histories. Two foxes are native to New England, the red and the gray. The gray fox is sometimes called the tree-climbing fox because it has the remarkable ability to climb trees with low branches. It is somewhat smaller than the red fox, and nowhere nearly as smart. But fox hunters have trouble getting a gray fox because when their dogs get close, the fox climbs a tree and the dogs lose the scent.

The red fox, the Reynard of folk tales, is one of the smartest of all animals. It actually seems to take pleasure in a chase by the hounds if it can get into the woodland or a brushy lot. It will leap to a stone wall and walk there to mask its trail. It will double back in its own tracks, leaving a dead end, then leap to one side and go another way. Having confused its pursuers, it will lie on a hillside and watch the confusion, as though laughing to itself.

The red fox is a skillful thief, and when every farmer kept a pen of chickens, it was a constant hazard to the flock. At times the fox will take newborn pigs and lambs. It seems to hate cats and quite often kills them. But it has what I can only call a sense of fun that delights me. Two examples:

One winter day when there was a light snow on the ground, I followed a fox track from its den to the stub railroad line that then crossed our farm. The fox was hunting, but evidently had time for diversion. It came to the railroad track, trotted along between the rails a little way, then got on one of the rails and tried to walk it, just as small boys occasionally did in my childhood. It walked that rail less than 100 yards, then fell off. The story was right there in the snow. It got on again, fell off again. This happened three times. Then it got the hang of it and walked that rail successfully for 200 yards. Then it deliberately stepped off and went its way.

One late summer day, about nine in the morning, Barbara called me from the kitchen. A fox was busy in the pasture grass just beyond our vegetable garden, not fifty yards from the house. It nosed the grass, paused, tensed, pounced, and came up with a field mouse in its jaws. A flip of its head, and it tossed the mouse into the air, watched where it fell, then edged close, tensed, pounced again. Again it tossed the mouse into the air. Three times it did this. Then the fourth time, and when it tossed the mouse upward, the fox opened its mouth wide, caught the falling mouse, gulped, and the game was over. It trotted back across the home pasture toward the wooded hillside.

I have no doubt that the early settlers tried to wipe out the foxes. One of the early leaders once said, "Animals and birds that cannot be eaten are worthless and should be destroyed," a policy still advocated by the more rabid anti-conservationists. But the foxes weren't easily destroyed. If anything, they have increased in numbers and grown smarter over the years. They probably will outlast man.

The coyote, that other cousin of the wolf, is not a native of New England or of any eastern region. The western prairies and high plains are the coyote's homeland. (And before I go one word further, I must say firmly that a coyote is a "Ky-Oat," not a "Ky-Otee." That "ee" ending, which is heard insistently on radio and television and in motion pictures, is never used in high plains coyote country. It is a California term, and ranks with such words as "doggie" and "horsie" in the childish vocabulary. The original Aztec name was *Coyotl*.)

In recent years the coyote, which is at least as clever as the red fox, has spread eastward, all the way to the Northeast. For a time it was believed that specimens trapped or shot here in the East were cross-bred animals, half dog, half coyote, though nobody could say where the coyotes came from to breed. They were called "coy-dogs." Then coyotes were identified here in New England, pure-blood coyotes; but they were bigger and heavier than the western coyotes. This was the result of a better diet, some biologists say. More rabbits, maybe, and fewer grasshoppers.

We now have at least one family of these bigger coyotes within a few miles of where I live. They appropriated and remodeled an old woodchuck den in an open field near a thin woodland. They were first sight-identified, then identified by their night calling, by the warden at a nearby nature reservation who spent a number of years in the National Park Service in coyote country.

New England has quite a few black bears, mostly in the more remote areas of Vermont, New Hampshire, and Maine. Now and then one of them strays down to western Massachusetts or my corner of Connecticut, always with a blare of publicity and a touch of wide-eyed fear. Few people seem to know that, unless it is a female with cubs, the worst a bear will do is batter a garbage can and break down a fence in panicked flight if it sees or hears a human being. And females with cubs almost never go wandering. They have a home territory and they tend to stay there. The wanderers usually are old boars with bad teeth and a poor sense of direction. They may be short-tempered, and any angry or confused bear can be dangerous. But those wanderers seldom stay long in any one place.

One of those wandering bears came though our area a few years ago and I saw its tracks in the mud along the riverbank. But I didn't see the bear, and two days later one was reported thirty miles northwest of here. Probably the same bear.

New England still has her share of birds and animals, both those that prefer to live near people and those that are persistently wild. Of the original inhabitants, however, quite a few have been wiped out or have gone elsewhere—the great auk, the wild turkey, the heath hen, the passenger pigeon, the wolf, the panther, the woods bison, the elk, the caribou.

37

38

39

40

41

CHAPTER 6

IF I HAD GROWN UP almost anywhere but on the high, dry plains of the West, I probably would better appreciate New England's seashore. There are more than 6,000 miles of it; and when you realize that the whole Atlantic coast, from the upper tip of Maine to the lower tip of Florida, has only 28,673 miles of seashore, that's a lot of coves and inlets, headlands and harbors. I have walked a good many miles of sandy New England beaches and rocky shorelines, but surf and salt water do not rouse me to ecstasy as they do Barbara, my wife. She grew up swimming in salt water and must see the ocean and smell the salt marshes now and then or feel dismally deprived. That is the reason I know something about the New England coast. I have been sunburned on Connecticut beaches while she swam, have counted countless gulls and sandpipers on Cape Cod's dunes while she bathed, have been frozen rigid standing knee-deep in the waters of Maine while she and various mermaids and mermen frolicked in the coldest surf this side of Spitzbergen.

I do like to sail a small boat and like to think I have a moderate degree of skill at it, though I am what must be called a "pond sailor." But once I sailed a small boat offshore in Maine and even brought it safely back to its own dock. I have been subjected to rough water and weather on seagoing fishing boats, but have never been seasick. Maybe I can be trusted to discuss some aspects, then, of New England's maritime history and experience.

All the early colonies were inevitably coastal communities. The colonists came by ship, had to find a place to disembark, and wouldn't have lugged their gear far inland even if they had been sure the woods weren't full of blood-thirsty Indians and man-eating wolves, bears, and woodchucks. So all the early settlements were on the water.

The colonies were established to make a profit for their backers, and one of the first profitable enterprises was fishing. The men who could be taught to catch codfish were set to work, and cod were dried and shipped back to Europe. The fishermen learned to sail boats, eventually learned to build them. So the cod bred the maritime experience which was to make New England the center of shipping and oceanic trade and transport for years.

By the eighteenth century, Yankee ships had become the carriers for virtually all the English colonies here. They took tobacco from Virginia, grain from the mid-Atlantic colonies, sugar from the West Indies, to England; and they carried back manufactured goods and luxuries for colonial planters and merchants. But England had her own shipping to protect, so she forbade American colonial trade with countries other than England. To get around this the colonial shipping men developed what was called the Triangular Trade. They took lumber, codfish, and livestock to the West Indies, sold them there, and brought back sugar and molasses. The molasses was made into rum, and the rum was taken to Africa and traded for slaves; the slaves were brought back to the West Indies and sold to sugar producers there for gold. And finally, the gold was taken to England and used to buy English luxuries and other manufactured goods for the American colonial market.

This sounds like a mixed-up, complicated way to do business, and it was. The Yankee ship men kept it complicated because it was illegal, and the English didn't seem able to unravel the details and put a stop to it. The English authorities here in America didn't try very hard, to tell the truth. In a sense, it was smuggling, and quite a few large family fortunes were founded on it. No doubt a good deal of hush money was paid, too.

Finally the long-standing rivalry between England and France culminated in what is now called The Seven Years' War, or the French and Indian War, 1756-1763. Much of the action was in America, where the French and their Indian allies persistently raided back-country New England. Despite such raids Yankee ship captains continued to trade with the French on such a scale that the whole British navy couldn't put a stop to it.

Out of this situation came English reform of colonial administration as well as the Sugar Act and the Stamp Act and new import duties on items such as paint, glass, and tea. This added fire to the smoldering rebellion that eventually flamed into the Revolution. So in one sense, those fishermen who caught and dried codfish should get credit for American independence. They started the early colonists on the way to becoming sailors and shipbuilders. Shipping became the major economic factor and the major means of trade for the New England colonies. They were the economic center for the whole American colonial establishment, and when the mother country tried to curb that trade, the colonists rebelled. Led, I might note, by a vigorous group of rebels in and around Boston.

After the war, shipping swiftly expanded, especially that centered on Boston and Cape Cod. Coastal New Englanders, and especially Cape Codders, became internationally famous ship captains. They had learned their trade in coastal traffic. Now they became trans-Atlantic traders, then began to round Cape Horn and take a hand in the fur trade of the American Northwest. From there they reached across the Pacific to the Spice Islands, the East Indies, for which the early explorers had been looking when they found America barring their way.

These Yankee captains, some of them still in their early twenties, sailed their snub-nosed old schooners quite profitably for half a century before the speeding world began to think in terms of hours and minutes rather than days and weeks. Then, in 1841, a New York marine architect named Joseph Griffeths designed a ship that was to change the whole picture. The Griffeths ship was "long, lean, and rakish, with hollow cheeks," as some described it, a hull shaped like a codfish instead of a sperm whale. Soon all the new ships approximated those lines and the Age of the Clippers was here.

That was the golden age of the sailing ship. It lasted only a short time, really, less than twenty years. But American clipper captains became internationally known. There is no complete list of them, but such a roll certainly would include these names: Captains Watson Chadwick, Rowland Crocker, Ezra Nye, the Bursley brothers Ira and Allen, Franklin Hallett, Allen H. Knowles, Jabez Howes, John Collins, the three Eldridge brothers John, Asa, and Oliver, Joshua Sears, and Elkanah Crowell.

Then came the American Civil War, and after that the steamships began to ply the ocean lanes. By the 1880s the great days of sail were over. By the end of the century Boston had become a secondary port. But the great days of sail, the heyday of the ocean voyagers with their endlessly varied cargoes, had given New England, and particularly Massachusetts, a perspective on the world that no other area ever achieved. Those Yankee captains and their crews knew more about far places and strange people than those responsible for our international affairs in Washington. It may well be that they were more broad-minded about such matters, too.

The end of those now almost legendary years of shipping, however, made no real change in this New England seashore. A few piers, a few shipyards, a good many cheap saloons and brothels were closed and eventually forgotten. But the headlands and the inlets, the salt marshes and the coves remained intact until well into the present century, when entrepreneurs big and little began filling the marshes and "reclaiming" the coves for factory sites and suburban or recreational housing. This has roused the environmentalists to action, and we may yet be able to save enough to remind our grandchildren that there was a time when we had a beautiful coastline all along the New England shore.

This is the most rugged coastline in the United States, with Maine providing the greater part of it and, quite definitely, the most rocky and uncompromising part. This coastline is so rugged because it is what geologists call a "drowned" coast. About 200 million years ago, a gigantic uplift of the earth's crust created a tremendous mountain range whose remnants today are known as the Appalachians. Weathering and erosion eventually wore down the mountains here in the Northeast to a plateau with only a few higher ridges and peaks of tough, resistant rock, what we now know as the Green and White Mountains and a few such lone mountains as Katahdin. Over this plateau, and eventually in deep valleys there, flowed the streams that once had rushed down the mountainsides, slowly grinding the valleys deeper and deeper.

Then, about sixty million years ago, the land was tilted to the east and south, perhaps in the same convulsions that thrust the Rocky Mountains to their great height. This set the streams in the New England area flowing swiftly again, carving and gullying the softer rock and leaving the tougher granite ridges. Eventually the outwash of those streams formed the coastal plain and became sedimentary rock, and New England had a broad, flat coastal plain much like that today from New Jersey southward.

Then came the ice. It came down from the north, and an eastern arm of it spread over New England, as I described earlier. The tremendous weight of the ice, two miles thick in places, depressed and compacted the land beneath it, so that when the ice eventually melted and the oceans rose, the coastal plain in New England was submerged. Today it is only a few fathoms under water, but it extends 100 miles out into the Atlantic and creates the once-fabulous fishing grounds of the Grand Banks.

But the point is that in thus "drowning" the coastal plain, the ocean reached those old worn-down mountains and their deep-cut valleys that today are the rocky eminences and the islands and the countless inlets and harbors along this whole coast.

New England's coastal plain is the continental shelf and under water. Its wealth of good harbors fostered seafaring, shipbuilding, and fishing.

The environment always shapes the lives and characters of its people to some extent. The people of the South and Southeast were shaped by cotton and tobacco before the South became industrial. Those of the Midwest, both farmers and townsmen, have been shaped by corn and hogs and the farms that produced them. The people of my native High Plains were shaped first by cattle, later by wheat.

Incidentally, when I see photographs of clipper ship captains or meet a veteran seafaring man out of a New England port, I think of the old cattlemen I knew as a boy. It is in the face and eyes that I see a resemblance. Both have that far-away look, the eyes seeming to look beyond, toward a distant horizon. And time after time I have seen, in both of them, those habitually lowered eyelids, even in shadow, the long-habitual guard against the glare of vast skies and unbroken horizons. They are the only people in whom I have ever seen that look, the far-roaming seafarer and the horseman of the trail-herds and the open range. Seeing them, I remember the vast sea of grass there was before the plowmen opened it to the eroding winds, a dry-land sea remotely comparable to the vastness of the salt water seas.

As I noted in an earlier chapter, the coastal waters of New England were teeming with fish when the first Europeans arrived. Over the years, fishing continued to be an important part of the area's economy, until after World War II. Then the tremendous increase in world population and the widespread demand for a higher standard of living began to deplete what had always been considered an inexhaustible ocean food supply. Fishing fleets from Russia and Japan primarily, but also from the lesser nations, reduced the number of whales to a dangerously low point, pretty well cleaned out the cod from the Grand Banks and made serious inroads on all the traditional fishing grounds. Our own fishermen found their hauls steadily diminishing, perhaps in part from overfishing but also from the effects of widespread pollution. In addition to sewage, which had fouled the rivers and the oceans at their mouths since time immemorial, the rivers now were poisoned with pesticides and chemical fertilizers, run off from farm fields and woodlands. With DDT now found in the Antarctic Ocean, we can hardly expect our coastal waters to be free of it. And such persistent chemical poisons sicken and sterilize fish and shellfish.

Thirty years ago we ate lobsters caught in the waters off Connecticut, in the area below New Haven. They were of excellent flavor and reminded Barbara of lobsters they had in the same area when she was a small girl and her family summered at the shore. In those days, a neighboring family of year-rounders fished commercially for lobsters, she recalls, cooked them, removed the meat, and sold it for a fancy price, perhaps as much as seventy-five cents a pound. She, with childish duplicity, cultivated a friendship with the family's grubby youngest daughter, about her own age, so she could have a share of the lobster legs. The legs have a tiny bit of meat in them, not enough for grown-ups to bother with; but to Barbara it was ambrosia. It still is. I sometimes think we pay extortionate prices for Maine lobsters, when they are available at all, just so she can suck those soda-straw legs.

I doubt that any family makes a living today catching lobsters off the Connecticut shore. They are getting scarce even in Maine. But the lobster fishermen still work at their trade, most of them from boats driven by outboard motors. A few years ago, however, I saw one lobsterman in cove water near Boothbay whom I shall never forget. He was a tall, lean, leathery man and he was standing in his boat as he rowed out to tend his shallow-water traps. Yes, standing. That is what made me look not twice but three times. It was the first time I'd ever seen a man row a boat standing up. His oarlocks were on posts about waist-high and he rowed facing forward, pushing his oars instead of pulling them. I never got to talk to him, but I was told that this arrangement is not unique. It enables a man to see better than when he is sitting down in the traditional position. But it is used only in relatively calm water, as in coves and harbors. Outside, where the water can get rough, they use bigger boats, often with cabins, or conventional rowboats.

I spoke earlier of the extent of New England's shoreline. Maine is the outstanding example of the jagged stretch of bays and promontories. Bee-line, Maine is only about 230 miles north to south. But a line tracing all the coves, inlets, and harbors stretches that distance over sixteen times, to 3,750 miles. Even the Massachusetts coastline, which is nowhere near so jagged, is almost eleven times its overall length, bee-line.

Cape Cod and Nantucket, Martha's Vineyard and all the small nearby islands, as well as Long Island, are children of the Ice Age. They are huge piles of clay, stones, boulders, and sand carried by the ice and dropped on what now are the submerged banks of the continental shelf. Boston originally was an Ice Age creation, an area covered with egg-shaped glacial hills called *drumlins*. Most of those drumlins have been leveled to fill tidal marshes and provide room for the city's growth. All cities do this. It long has been called progress to cut down a hill or fill a valley or a coastal marsh. But Bunker Hill and Breed's Hill, well-remembered in the history of the Revolutionary War, both are drumlins. Several others persist in Boston Harbor, thrusting up from the water like the humped backs of huge dolphins.

Cape Cod, which reaches fifty miles out into the Atlantic, is a kind of climate buffer. The water on the north side of the Cape averages ten degrees colder than that on the south side, which is moderated by the Gulf Stream farther to the south. Even the plants and animals are somewhat different, above and below the Cape. And there is a remarkable difference in the tides. Above the Cape are some of the highest tides in the world. In the Bay of Fundy, for example, tides may reach as much as fifty feet, and this influences tides all the way down the coast and into Cape Cod Bay. At Calais, Maine, on the New Brunswick border, tides run as high as twenty-two feet. On the bayside of Cape Cod they average about ten feet. Just across the Cape, on the south side, they run only about two feet. And at Nantucket, the tide normally rises only about a foot and a half.

Those cold tides inevitably chill the air, so the Maine coast has, and apparently has had since the Ice Age, conifer forests, primarily balsam fir and spruce. Balsam fir can live right down to the water, and often does. But red spruce, common just a little way inland, thins out as it nears the ocean, and white spruce takes its place at the edge of the sea. Spruce is shallow-rooted, can live right on the rocks and actually lean out over the water. Its roots will reach out and find just enough soil to keep it alive. So most of Maine's rugged coastline and most of its larger islands are green with spruce. Farther inland, the pines, especially white pines, predominate, along with oaks and maples.

Now I find that I have discussed the Maine coast, though by no means exhaustively, and have paid a landsman's respects to Cape Cod and the Boston area. But I haven't even mentioned Salem and that famous rock. We have friends there, and we appreciate the place and its history. But I, for one, can think of better places for newcomers to have landed. That, of course, is hindsight. If I had been on that ship, no doubt I would have been glad to get ashore anywhere.

I haven't mentioned Gloucester and its famous fishing fleet of the recent past. The last time we were there the odors from its nearby salt marshes were rank with something other than seawater. But the old piers and docks and the fishing boats tied up there still had that unforgettable look of the fabulous past.

I haven't mentioned Rockport or Cape Ann, which the natives think of in the same breath, so to speak, with Gloucester. Gloucester and Rockport comprise the rocky peninsula of Cape Ann, occupy it completely. The Cape has a seafaring tradition that reaches back more than 300 years, to the Dorchester Adventurers' colony established there in 1623. And the aroma I just spoke of is described locally as the smell of tar, salt air, and codfish drying in the sun. For a long time, Rockport has been a favorite summer haven for artists, and recently the area has become quite special for nonartists who simply want to live within sight and smell of the ocean.

I would say the same pleasant thing about all these places—they have the wonderful old seaport smell, even when there isn't a salt marsh nearby. And they have a longer white-man history than most, though not all, other places in this country. I do make exceptions. The Spanish founded St. Augustine, Florida, in 1565, and Santa Fe, New Mexico, in 1609.

For that matter, I haven't mentioned Rhode Island, which has only 40 miles of coastline but 348 miles of shoreline. Those terms are not synonymous. The coastline is the general outline of the seacoast, but the shoreline takes in bays, rivers, inlets, and all such places up to the point where tidewater ends or narrows to 100 feet or less. Anyway, Rhode Island has beautiful beaches along its little stretch of seacoast. And for many years those beaches were the pride and joy of a special breed of New Englanders. Rhode Islanders were ranchmen and dairymen, of all things, and grew sheep, cattle, and horses. They even developed a special breed of horses, the Narragansett pacers. They had dairies that milked as many as 100 cows, and they made a special kind of Cheshire cheese. The leading families lived like the Carolina tobacco planters, in huge houses, in elegant dress, with rare wines, elaborate meals, Negro and Indian slaves. They were a horsey crowd, lived lavishly, and were especially proud of their beaches. Eventually they had to do without their slaves, had to accept industry, and quieted down somewhat. But they never were as sedate as Boston's hymn-singers or as fanatic as Connecticut's Puritan pioneers. And their beaches were the playground for the latter-day social leaders from Boston and New York. Roger Williams left quite a legacy.

I've barely mentioned that Connecticut has a seacoast. It has, a perfectly good seacoast; but it isn't exciting, even to the natives. In a general description of Connecticut forty years ago by the Federal Writers' Project, this was the sum of its comment on that subject:

> The state's coastal plain, extending along Long Island Sound, is well developed commercially and residentially. Seaside resorts, state parks, and

bathing beaches line the shore, with some intervening marshland. There are several good harbors. . . Shipping was once of great importance, but it is now relatively negligible except for coastwise traffic.

There was shipbuilding at Derby, at the head of tidewater on the Housatonic River, as early as 1657. New Haven became the state's major port after the Revolution, with a flourishing trade to China and the East Indies early in the 1800s. A sailing fleet operated out of New Haven and a whaling fleet out of New London in the 1850s and 1860s. Shipyards at Mystic were noted for their clipper ships.

Now the days of sail are past and the old shipyards are gone. The fishing fleets are reduced to relatively few vessels. The rivers that pour their waters into the ocean are filthy with humanity's waste, fouling and poisoning harbors and beaches.

But the seashore, the vastness of the ocean, the inevitability of the tides, are still fascinating. We go there today to see and hear and feel the certainties that are beyond human reach. Perhaps that is why this coastline is so rugged. Perhaps that is why New England is the way it is. I know that I, plainsman born and raised, stand in awe and reverence on the beach and watch the surf endlessly roll in from the farthest reaches of the earth.

47

48

CHAPTER 7

THERE ARE THE LEGENDS and the tales and the people, and here are a few as I have heard them:

Charley Fuller was an independent man who lived alone just above Schenob Swamp. He was slim as your finger, said my friend Morris who told me about him, a little bit of a man, but tough as rawhide. Even as an old man—he lived into his nineties—he had phenomenal eyes. He would sit and watch the ledges on the mountains called Plantain and Race, across the valley, and he would say, "I'll be back," and pick up his rifle and just drift off across the valley toward the place he had seen a fox lying up. He might be gone three hours, but he would come back with the fox. He was a remarkable still hunter. In winter he would go out alone in the snow, with no dog, and find a fox track and follow it half a day. Eventually he would get a shot. One shot was all he needed.

Charley Fuller was a carpenter by trade, and a good one, but when he took a job he warned you, "If it comes up a shower I'll be leaving." He meant that if it rained he was going fishing, to catch them on the water's rise. He knew every nook and cranny of the swamp and its brooks, and he caught trout in there that ran to three and four pounds. He was a worm fisherman, one of the best. He had a tiny fish tattooed on his chest. But he never ate fish. He gave them away.

Those were the days when there were lake trout, big ones, in Wononscopomuc (the Lakeville lake here in the corner of Connecticut). Charley Fuller knew that lake as he knew the palm of his hand. He once caught five lake trout, the legal limit for one day, and the smallest ran close to fifteen pounds. The biggest one, the biggest he ever took in Wononscopomuc, weighed just over twenty-six pounds. He told of the time when he hooked one even bigger. "Must have been close to fifty pounds," he said. But he never landed it. For those big fish, he baited with suckers eight or ten inches long.

And Charley was a trapper. He once caught five otters in one day, and nobody ever tried to count the muskrats he took. Hiram Beebe, who used to buy fur in Canaan, Connecticut, once said he had bought more than sixty thousand dollars' worth of fur from Charley Fuller, over the years.

Charley Fuller died more than thirty years ago, and Schenob Swamp has changed a good deal since then. Beavers have been at work in there, and they change any water they take over. Nobody even today knows all the secrets of that swamp, where mosquitoes big as hummingbirds take over every summer. Maybe some of those big trout are still there. Charley Fuller was the only one who ever took many of them. If he came back today you can be sure he would soon find out if they are there. It wouldn't take Charley Fuller long to learn the secrets of Schenob Swamp again.

><

John Chapman was born about 1775, either in Boston or in Springfield, Massachusetts. Nobody knows much about his early life, except that even as a boy he wandered off on long trips in search of birds or flowers. He seems to have had little education. In his early twenties he passed a cider mill in Pennsylvania, saw all the seeds in the pomace, the leftover pulp, and took a pailful of it into the woods and planted it. Apple trees grew from the seeds, and he soon became "Johnny Appleseed," the strange wanderer who planted apple trees all through the Ohio Country.

He was first seen there in 1801, near Steubenville, in twin canoes lashed together, one of them full of seedy apple pomace. He kept planting orchards and seedlings from his wilderness orchards, and he made the rounds each year, pruning and caring for the trees. He also planted herbs, catnip, pennyroyal, horehound, and even dog fennel, which he believed cured malaria. The Indians knew him and regarded him as a medicine man of great power.

He visited early settlers' cabins, gave them apple trees and herbs, and read the Bible to them in a resounding voice. He was accepted as a kind of border saint, and he was kind to animals to a fanatic degree, refusing even to kill insects or poisonous snakes.

He once attended a frontier revival meeting at which the gospel-shouting preacher demanded, "Where is the man who, like the primitive Christian, walks toward heaven barefoot and clad in sack-cloth?" And Johnny Appleseed, wearing stagged-off old trousers and a meal sack with holes cut for head and arms as a shirt, barefoot, unshaven and unshorn, a tin mush-pan on his head for a hat, went down the aisle to the pulpit and shouted, "Here is a primitive Christian!"

He continued to plant and tend his wilderness orchards, and act as a missionary wherever he went, until the spring of 1847, when he caught pneumonia and died in a frontier settler's cabin in what is now Allen County, Indiana.

❧

I never met W. A. "Snowflake" Bentley, but I have talked with several people who knew him—not intimately, but to talk to. Nobody knew Mr. Bentley intimately. There was, and still is, some doubt whether his first name was Wilson or Winton. He always signed as W. A. Bentley. The A stood for Alwyn. He was shy, laconic, and a stranger even to his Vermont neighbors, who couldn't see why anybody should think snow-flakes were beautiful or want to spend his life studying them. He once was persuaded to give a talk in his native village about his snowflake studies and, so the story goes, only six persons went to hear him. But when he died in 1931, at the age of sixty-six, he was known by name and work in learned circles all over the United States and abroad. He left more than five thousand snowflake negatives, a unique collection. About twenty-five hundred of them were published the year of his death in a volume titled simply *Snow Crystals*.

He was born the year the Civil War ended, on a farm in the town of Jericho, Vermont, midway between Burlington, on Lake Champlain, and Mount Mansfield. This is the long-winter area, where the season's snowfall averages ten feet. His father was a farmer, making a skimpy living on the stony land. His mother had been a schoolteacher and apparently gave young Bentley all the education he ever had. He grew up as most farm boys did, taking the place of a hired hand as soon as he could reach the plow handles and had hands big enough to milk a cow. But he had intense curiosity about everything around him, which his mother fostered. Eventually she scrimped enough money to buy him a crude telescope. He used the lenses to examine everything from pollen to rocks, and one winter day looked through them at a snowflake on his dark coatsleeve. He discovered the ice crystal.

After that he wanted a camera and a microscope, and somehow his parents scraped up the money to buy them. He began making pictures of snowflakes. He used the same camera and scope for fifty years, developing his own technique for handling snowflakes, which required working in the open woodshed in temperatures below freezing. The only existing picture of him at work shows him with heavy winter mittens but wearing a Fedora hat, a Chesterfield overcoat, a high, stiff linen collar, and a necktie. He remained on the family farm all his life. There was no snow during a farmer's busy months, and no good Yankee could sit idle, so he farmed. He never married.

He once said, "Some folks call me crazy. They want to know what good it does to get all those pictures of just snow. I don't argue with them. I am satisfied. I have got letters from men with lots of letters after their names who know a hundred times more than I do, or anyone around here, I guess. And those men tell me I am doing a great work. I don't know about that, but I do know what I like. And I think I see as much around here to enjoy, right here on my own farm, as those who call me a fool. Most of them have never seen a darned thing."

❧

Justin Morgan was the name first of a man, then of a horse. The horse is better remembered, but both their ancestries were obscure. Both were Yankees.

Justin Morgan, the man, was born about 1747, in or near West Springfield, Massachusetts. He was a sickly child who became a sickly man, too frail for physical labor. He got a public school education, and from time to time all his life gave lessons in singing and penmanship, as a kind of private tutor. For a time he ran a wayside tavern, and then for several years he had charge of horses kept for stud service. In 1788, he moved to Randolph, Vermont, about midway between Rutland and Montpelier, where he was elected lister and later town clerk.

His wife died three years later, leaving four small children, who were parceled out to neighbors. His family broken up, Justin Morgan drifted from one neighborhood to another, barely eking out a living. In 1795, he went back to West Springfield to try to collect a debt long owed him for tutoring. He collected, but instead of money had to take two young horses, one a big, good-looking gelding, the other a runty and ungelded bay. He sold the big gelding, but for some reason kept the little bay colt, which he called his "Dutch horse." When Morgan died three years later, he willed this horse to his friend William Rice in Woodstock, Vermont, at whose home he had spent his last, dying days.

And now the horse.

The little bay was known only as "Justin Morgan's horse" at first, and eventually as

Justin Morgan. He was actually little more than pony size, a bit over fourteen hands (fifty-six inches) at the shoulder and weighing less than one thousand pounds. He was thick-set, docile, quick, energetic, seemed almost tireless, and could outpull some of the largest horses around. Rice kept him only a short while, then sold him. He was leased to various farmers, who used him in the fields and the woods, as a buggy horse and a saddle horse, and bred their mares to him. He was sold again, and again, and each new owner was surprised at what he could do. Eventually he grew old, and at the age of twenty-nine he died.

Justin Morgan, the horse, left a good many offspring, colts that matured into small, tough, energetic horses. Soon it was obvious that he had been one of those rare animals with the genetic power to project his own characteristics through succeeding generations. His offspring, when cross-bred, eventually produced a distinct type of horse with many desirable traits and abilities. By the middle of the nineteenth century, the Morgan horse had become widely known as a general-purpose horse, attractive in appearance, gentle to handle, excellent for riding or driving or any farm task. Eventually, the U.S. Department of Agriculture and the Vermont State Experiment Station assembled a small band of Morgans at Burlington, Vermont, to perpetuate the breed. Today there is extensive record-keeping to keep the blood lines clear, and Justin Morgan, both man and horse, are well remembered. Morgan horses today are known all over the world.

ac

Some called him a "professional Yankee," but that was unjust. He was born in Newton Center, Massachusetts, and was a graduate of Harvard. He lived much of his life in Dublin, New Hampshire, and was a selectman there as well as moderator. He was tall and lean and he developed a drawling, somewhat nasal way of Yankee speech.

His name was Robb Sagendorph but he masqueraded as Abe Weatherwise, a rhymester and weather forecaster for *The Old Farmer's Almanac,* which he took over in the 1930s as a dying publication. By all logic, the *Almanac* should have been put out of business by the Weather Bureau and the availability of calendars and star charts. But he tapped a vein of nostalgia and gave it new life. Deeply interested in weather and meteorology, he expanded the old guesswork into shrewd analysis of norms, averages, and possibilities. For years he based his forecasts on sunspots, weather cycles, and careful analysis, covering his tracks with a gloss of humor. On the whole, he did better than official long-range forecasters, averaging around 70 percent accuracy. The *Almanac* throve, and he started a monthly magazine, *Yankee.* It throve, too.

In the 1950s, he asked me to write a set of short verses for the *Almanac,* one for each month. I wrote these verses several years, then asked for a raise. He promised me one. The next year he raised the payment by $1.20, ten cents a verse. I phoned him and snorted loudly. He laughed, said something about "a good Yankee trick." I wrote no more verses, and our friendship cooled.

One night two years later, he telephoned me. That in itself was phenomenal. He almost never made a toll call when a letter would suffice. Or a post card, which cost even less.

He phoned me, and his voice was hoarse, seemed about to break. He had just finished reading the book about my dog, Pat. His own dog had died only a few weeks before. He started to tell me about his dog, a long, rambling tale of companionship and affection. But he choked, said, "You understand. I know you understand," and had to hang up. Two days later I received a longhand letter written immediately after the phone call. Like the call, it was from the heart.

We never mentioned either phone call or the letter. Or for that matter, his dog or mine. We were back on that plane of casual friendship, he playing the crafty, sharp-dealing Yankee, I the half-innocent outlander niggling over dimes. I wrote a couple of articles for his magazine and without argument he paid me a shade over the going rate.

A few years ago I had another handwritten letter from him, this one quite brief. He wasn't feeling well. He wasn't sure he would ever feel well again, or that he wanted to. The next word I had was of his death.

⁊C

He was born in Massachusetts but was taken, as a small child, to Virginia. He was up this way on a vacation trip and had always wanted to see this valley. He stopped in, and within five minutes wanted to look at our old apple trees, since he lives in the Shenandoah Valley, apple country. So we went out and looked, and he shook his head sadly. "Those trees," he said, "need pruning. Much too tall. You can't pick them."

"We don't keep them for fruit," I said. "We keep them for blossoms. We get all the fruit we want, and leftovers for the deer."

"How often do you spray?"

"We don't."

"Lots of drops, then."

"Sure they drop. Woodchucks eat them. And deer, as I said."

He smiled and shook his head. "You aren't an apple man."

"Definitely not. I like apple jelly and applesauce. But mostly we like apple blossoms."

He sighed. "Down my way we grow apples for market. Spray them. Keep the trees low. Prune them. But," he admitted, "we still don't have apples like we used to have."

"I wondered if you would admit that."

"Well, it's the truth. They've bred apples up, made them pretty. Put color into them, made them uniform in size, developed better keeping quality. We ship them all over the country. But, you know, I wish I'd come when your apples are ripe. They must have flavor."

"Quite a bit. Sometimes you have to watch out for worms, though. But they make excellent jelly. The apples, I mean."

He picked up a small, green, immature apple, held it in his hand. "My grandfather had a farm over near Worcester. I used to go there sometimes in late summer. They made their own cider and vinegar and apple butter, from their own apples. The apples weren't pretty, but they did have some taste to them." He sighed. "Apples weren't a business then."

He tossed away the little green apple in his hand and I could see that he had already forgotten those summers on his grandfather's farm. "You could still grow good apples," he said, "if you would prune and spray."

"I don't want good apples. If I had a crop of good apples I'd have to pick them, pack them, sell them. I'd have to build a storage place and—No, I don't want to get into that business!"

"You could make cider."

"If I made cider, I'd have to make vinegar. And I would want to make Stone Fence, as they used to call it. Applejack has its virtues, but you can't drink more than a few gallons a year, and if you try to sell it you've got revenue officers on your neck. I've got enough trouble now. Besides, those aren't very good cider apples."

"No, I guess not. You know what I'd do with this place? I'd set out young Macs and Red Delicious, and when they started bearing I'd cut down the old trees."

"I don't particularly like Macs or Red Delicious."

"They sell well."

I didn't answer. He tried once more. "Or you could keep bees. Apple blossoms make fine honey."

"I've got a swarm. Wild ones. In that big maple over there. It's hollow. The bees have a ball when the apple trees come to bloom."

"Make a lot of honey?"

"You don't think I'd cut down that maple to find out, do you?"

He sighed and shook his head. "No, I guess not."

We went back to the house and he got his hat and pretty soon he said goodbye and drove away.

æ

There are so many tales about Ethan Allen it's hard to choose among them. There's the one, for instance, about his last Thanksgiving here in Salisbury. This was before there was an official Thanksgiving, but facts never could stand in the way of a good story about Old Ethan.

Ethan wanted roast goose for his Thanksgiving dinner, it seems. So he took his gun and went down to Lake Wononscopomuc. There was a flock of geese there, about halfway across the lake, but Ethan honked like a gander and lured them closer. They came up within 200 yards and Ethan shot a fine young goose. Then he stripped and swam out and got it, the water being open, with only a fringe of ice around the edges.

He got his goose and gathered a few friends and went to the inn up the road and told the cook there just how he wanted his goose cooked. Then he and his friends had a few drinks and got to frolicking. But before they tore the place apart, Ethan got them all to enlist, and then and there created his army, the Green Mountain Boys. Then they went on drinking and frolicking, and when the goose was ready to eat, Ethan was the only one still on his feet. So Ethan ate the goose, right down to the breastbone and wingtips.

By then the rest of the boys, Ethan's army, had slept it off. So he routed them out, mustered them into ranks, and headed north, toward Vermont, telling everyone in hearing that, in the name of God and the Continental Congress, he was going to capture that Godbedamned British fort at Ticonderoga.

And he did, didn't he?

Ethan, who believed in reincarnation, said he would come back in the form of a big white stallion. Sometimes on a moonless night I drive down the Lower Road in North Canaan, past the old furnace that Ethan once had a share of, and I stop and listen.

Sometimes I hear something that isn't the wind and isn't the waterfall in the Blackberry River, but just might be the neighing of a horse. The more I listen, the more sure I am. I turn off the motor and get out of the car, and sometimes I can actually *feel* the thud of hoofs in the open pasture nearby.

I have never seen him, but I keep listening and watching. Maybe next time, I tell myself, I shall see that big white stallion.

53

54

55

56

57

58

CHAPTER 8

IT SEEMS IMPOSSIBLE NOW, but the early colonists went hungry, almost without exception, for weeks and months. This new land had plenty of food, but it was strange food and most of the newcomers distrusted it. They were not used to living off the land. They had never eaten wild meat and few had eaten fresh fish. And their palates were accustomed to barley and oats, not to this strange grain the Indians grew. It all took getting used to.

But eventually they learned to eat and like venison and wild turkey, even as the Indians did. They found that fresh fish was more palatable than salted cod. And once they had tasted American clams, and oysters, and lobsters, they found them tasty, after the initial surprise had worn off.

They took a leaf from the Indians' cookbook and sampled wild greens when the springtime hungers gnawed at their vitals. They boiled dock and purslane and milkweed and the fiddleheads of ferns. They boiled the living daylights out of them, of course. That was the way country cooks treated their vegetables, right up through my own grandmother's day. But some of the good in them, some of the vitamins, persisted and helped to satisfy that vernal hunger. Before long they had seed from "back home" and planted lettuce and cucumbers and beets in their gardens. The beets were grown for their tops, which made a tasty boiled vegetable. The red roots, for which most beets are grown today, were thrown away or fed to the hogs.

One of the uses of pumpkins—or "pompions," as they were called—was for molasses and beer. To make molasses they simply boiled down pumpkin juice, and for beer they let that juice ferment. They also made wine from berry juice and brandy from peach juice. Peach trees and apple trees were brought from England and planted as soon as the settlers had become self-sustaining. The apples provided cider and applejack, and along with peaches and blackberries could be dried for winter keeping. The fruit helped alleviate the scurvy which was common in all the colonies every winter. So did onions, parsnips, turnips, and cabbage, when they were available. And to some extent the cider, beer, and wines helped. But nobody knew what caused scurvy, so the treatment was pretty much guesswork.

Add the nuts every autumn—hickory nuts, chestnuts, and walnuts or butternuts—and you have the bulk of available foods for the early New Englanders. These foods sufficed, since their austere religion discouraged luxuries. However, there were no hard and fast rules about how the food was to be cooked, and that is one of the areas where the pioneer women left enduring legacies. They cooked their vegetables to a tasteless mush, but they did invent pumpkin pie. They adapted Indian pemmican to their own palates and made mincemeat pies. They made chowders from fresh fish and from Indian corn, with their own onions and cabbages. They made puddings from Indian cornmeal and their own dried fruit.

One reason they were slow to accept venison and other wild meat was that at home, in Europe, wild game belonged to the crown and only poachers ever took it. Most people, even the farm folk, ate pork when they had meat, and usually it was salt-cured, since there was no such thing as refrigeration. The colonists were not skilled or even experienced as hunters, and their weapons were not designed for hunting deer. They were better for killing waterfowl, and waterfowl were less difficult to hunt, since they were present in huge flocks on almost every cove and backwater. So ducks and geese were often on the pioneer menus. As was seafood, which was plentiful and required few special skills to gather. Oysters and clams were there in the water, ready to pick up. So were crabs and lobsters. And fish swam in all the streams. It took a bit of getting used to, because in Europe fish was papist food. But a hungry Puritan eventually found that he could eat oysters or lobsters or even fresh cod any day in the week without paying tribute to the Pope. Fish and seafood still constitute an important item in the New Englander's diet.

There was very little beef. The first cattle brought to America were oxen and were brought here as draft animals. Milk cows were brought in later, but primarily for cheese making. Few people drank milk, and butter was used only by the prosperous few.

Almost all the milk went into a variation of English cheddar or was used in the form of fresh curds, by those who happened to own a cow. Only mature animals were butchered for their meat. They were small animals, nothing like today's Angus and

Herefords, and their meat undoubtedly was lean and tough. They were grass-fed, and soon there was a shortage of pasture for them near the original few colonies. That was one reason some of the early settlers at New Town, now Cambridge, were willing to move to new settlements in the upper Connecticut River Valley—grass had become scarce along the Charles River. Colonists in Rhode Island made out as well as they did because they early turned to "ranching." Instead of plowing and planting, they let their clearings grow up in native grass and put their herds of cattle and flocks of sheep on it. The animals throve, and the eccentric Rhode Islanders almost from the start dealt in beef and had time to enjoy life. Some of them, to be sure, had to do things the hard way and become dairymen. One family had a milking herd of 100 cows, and made cheese by the ton. The flocks of sheep were kept for their wool, not for mutton or lamb. They were sheared, their wool was sold, and the same sheep went back to pasture and grew another crop of wool.

The early documents have little to say about swine, but they soon became common in the colonies. It was only natural they should, for the woods were full of oaks and beeches, mast for all the pigs the colonists could muster. Pork, of course, was indispensable when those ingenious cooks started making their savory baked beans. I have wondered if baked beans weren't a chance discovery, made when a kettleful of bean soup almost boiled dry over the coals. Molasses could have been added as an afterthought, perhaps to mask the slight burned-bean flavor, if that is how it happened. I was almost exiled when I first put a splash or two of vinegar on New England baked beans to temper the too-sweet molasses taste. The sentence was commuted when I welcomed apple pie for breakfast.

I had thought the ranch-country breakfast of ham or sausage, eggs, flapjacks, and cooked fruit was plenty for any outdoor workingman. But the back-country breakfast of New England farm folk made it look like a mere snack, particularly in winter. This tradition reaches far back, to early colonial days, when breakfast in New England consisted of rye pudding and bread, or hasty pudding— Indian porridge—with pea or bean soup, or stew flavored with salt pork or salt fish. Dinner, in the middle of the day, consisted of more bean soup with pork and stewed peas, squash, turnips, onions, and any other vegetables available. Supper was much like breakfast, but with the addition of gingerbread, some kind of sweetened cake, and cheese and pie, all washed down with beer. Beer was drunk at all meals, even by children.

The various stews we eat today were, with few exceptions, inventions of early

Yankee cooks. Beef stew was a luxury dish because beef was scarce, and lamb was almost unknown on the menu. Beef pot roast was a special Yankee achievement and also a luxury dish because of the scarcity of beef. The beef available was tough, and the pot roast was cooked long and slowly, often with wine added to help tenderize it. Later cooks found that tomatoes not only added flavor but also helped break down the tough fibers in the meat. Both Yankee stew and Yankee pot roast involve subtleties of cooking beyond the skills of a westerner accustomed to treating his beef as an oven roast, a broiled steak, or batter-dipped chicken-fried steak. It was a long time before Yankee stockmen learned to fatten a steer on grain and get a tender steak or roast. So there were no Yankee steaks for the colonists, and the roasts were compromises between tough meat and open-hearth cookery, which encouraged long, leisurely simmering.

Modern New England is a land of inns, and the inns usually are known for their food. A recent directory of New England inns lists 225 that are open year-round. It is, of course, an incomplete list, as are all such, but it does indicate how this area caters to hungry wayfarers, whether skiers, fishermen, mountain viewers and climbers, or mere vacationers or weekenders. The inns feature their menus, since inn patrons traditionally are hungry. The cooking varies from French to Bavarian to Spanish to "traditional home cooking" and "old Yankee recipes." One Vermont inn rates this notice: "Good home cooking is the order of the day, with occasional rarities such as possum stew and roast woodchuck." Early New Englanders did not indulge in possum stew. The opossum, as was noted in an earlier chapter, remained below the Mason-Dixon line until recent years. Down there, however, back-country cooks have stewed and roasted possum for a long time. As for woodchuck, or groundhog, it has been roasted like lamb and eaten in New England from time to time since early colonial days. Why it isn't mentioned more often in the early accounts is a mystery to me.

Diet, it seems, always was related to medicine, or perhaps vice versa. Among the early "remedies" was the use of fox "oil," or fat, for earache. The testicles of beavers were fried and eaten as a cure for palsy. A good fat beaver tail was cooked and eaten as an aphrodisiac, and probably was frowned upon by the church. Incidentally, it was believed that a child was born on the same day of the week that it was conceived, and since sexual relations were forbidden on Sunday, any child born on Sunday was considered evidence of forbidden conduct. The situation of a pastor whose wife bore twins on a Sunday was, shall we say, compromising. But it did happen.

To get back to fat beaver tails, however, I have often wondered why the nineteenth-century trappers, the Mountain Men of the West, considered beaver tail a special dietary treat. None of them took wives along on their trapping expeditions, and few of them had access to Indian squaws, young and compliant or old and uninterested. Maybe, despite those Puritan dietary beliefs, the trappers actually liked the flavor of beaver tail.

It was also believed that wolf dung mixed with white wine was a specific for colic. Maybe the very thought of it made the colic victim feel better, enough better at least to make the medication unnecessary. It was also believed that a few vulture bones hung like a pendant around the neck would soon put an end to a headache. That sounds like an Indian remedy, and perhaps was adapted from one by the early colonists.

For inflammation of almost any kind, this concoction was recommended: "Take fine wheaten floure mixed with the yolke of an egge, honey, and a little saffron. This doth heale byles and such like sores, in children and old people, very well and quickly. Take crumbs of wheaten bread one pound and a halfe, barley meal 3 ij. Fennigreke and Linseed of each an ounce, the leaves of Mallowes, Violets, Dwale, Senegreene and Cotyledon, and one handful: boyle them in water and oyle untill they be tender: then stampe them small in a stone mortar, and add thereto the yolke of three eggs, oyle of Roses, and Oyle of Violets, ana 3 ij. Incorporate them all together, then add the juice of Nightshade, Plantaine, and Henbane, ana 3 ij. It easeth an Erysipelas, or Saint Anthony's fire, and all inflamations very speedily."

It seems, offhand, that it might be simpler just to put up with the inflammation. But I remember, when I think that way, that I owe my life to a slice or two of wheat bread. When I was a very small child I had an abscess on my neck that was brought to a head and cured by my grandmother, using a poultice of home-made wheat bread and milk. What else besides plain bread and milk she put into it, I never learned. But I hereby attest that the "wheaten floure" mixture does have potency.

Indian "tabaco," or Nicotiana, or Henbane of Peru, as it was variously called, had a variety of virtues. These were detailed by John Gerard early in the seventeenth century. Since tobacco is an important crop today in the Connecticut Valley, let's have a look at Gerard's report.

> It bringeth drowsiness, troubleth the senses, and maketh man as it were
> drunke by taking the fume only . . . The leaves thereof are a remedie for the
> paine of the head called the Megram or Migram, that hath been of long

continuance. . . . It mitigateth the paine of the gout, if it be roasted in hot embers, and applied to the grieved part. Four ounces of the juice hereof drunke procureth afterward a long and sounde sleepe. A friend affirmed that a strong countryman of middle age having a dropsie, took it, and being wakened out of his sleepe called for meat and drinke, and after that became perfectly cured. The same man reported that he had cured many countrymen of agues with the distilled water of the leaves drunke a little before the fit. It is good against poyson, and taketh away the malignitie, if the juice be given to drink, or the wounds made by venomous beasts be washed therewith. The dry leaves are used to be taken in a pipe set on fire and suckt into the stomacke, and thrust forth againe at the nostrils, against the paines in the head, rheums, aches in any part of the bodie, whereof soever the originall proceed. These leaves do palliate or ease for a time, but never perform any cure absolutely; for though they empty the body of humours, yet the cause of the grief cannot be so taken away.

I find an interesting footnote to the tobacco topic in a message from James Cudworth when he declined a request that he command a Plymouth force in an expedition against the Dutch in 1663.

My wife, as is well known to the whole town, is not only a weak woman, and has been all along; . . . Never a day passes but she is forced to rise at break of day, or before; she cannot lay for want of breath, and when she is up she cannot light a pipe of tobacco, but it must be lighted for her; and until she has taken two or three pipes for want of breath she is not able to stir, and she has never a maid.

If Dame Cudworth had consulted my doctor she would have been told she had a severe case of emphysema and had damn well better stop smoking that pipe. Her heart probably was acting up, too, though she wasn't saying much about that to her husband. She bore her troubles without too much complaint, though as he says they were "well known to the whole town."

Until just before the Civil War, New England was to a large degree self-sustaining. That is to say, her own farm crops were enough to feed her people. It was a close race, even then, between agriculture and industry, and from about the middle of the nineteenth century industry took the lead.

The years between 1830 and 1880 were the thriving times for agriculture in New

England. Today her farms are often called an outdated extravagance. Dairy farming dominates the agricultural industry. A likely index to the rise and fall of farming may be seen in what happened in Connecticut.

Farming throve directly in proportion to open land available. You don't grow foodstuff in the woodland. By 1860 Connecticut was about three-quarters open land. Then farm abandonment began, and after the Civil War it increased steadily. By 1910 the woodland that automatically reclaims abandoned farmland had spread until it covered 45 percent of the state. From 27 percent in 1860 to 45 percent in 1910 is quite a change. By 1955 the open farmland had shrunk to only 37 percent of the state's total area, and today at least three quarters of the state is covered with woodland, leaving only one quarter for the cities, suburbs, villages, and farms.

This, I say, is typical of all New England today–about three quarters of the whole area is wooded and hence not available for agriculture. Maine has the most woodland, always has had it, and has the least farmland, except in its "potato belt."

Even today, however, the remaining farms in Connecticut produce 25 to 30 percent of the food needed in the state, 100 percent of the potatoes, 92 percent of the eggs, 45 percent of the dairy products. It is hard to say what will happen in the next five or ten years; in 1970 the College of Agriculture at the University of Connecticut had an enrollment of only 382 students and by 1975 that figure had risen to 1,227–more than a threefold increase.

Government figures indicate that income per acre for farmers in this area is nearly twice the national average. For one thing, the farmers are surrounded by consumers. They sell a large share of their crops at retail in their own farm markets and most of the rest goes to nearby distributors. Also, they primarily produce special crops, vegetables, fruit, dairy products. All these require less land than small-grain farming such as wheat and oats, and they need more specialized care and less machine work than is used on the big acreages in the Corn Belt and Wheat Country. Milking machines, hay balers, and silage choppers have lessened the hand work on dairy farms, but not to the degree that chemical weed killers and outsize combine harvesters have reduced hand labor needed to raise corn and wheat.

In the past fifteen or twenty years Connecticut has lost about half its farmland. It has been absorbed by urban sprawl, by expanded highways, and by abandonment to natural growth, which produces what is called "sproutland" on the tax rolls. The land lost to suburbs and highways cannot be reclaimed as farmland, and the sproutland probably was abandoned by farmers because it lost its topsoil and wasn't worth plowing or seeding.

A good deal of the farmland, both in Connecticut and elsewhere in New England, has been taken over by gentlemen farmers, businessmen who have made their money elsewhere. Often they are willing to keep the farms running even at a loss. Indeed, often they welcome a loss for income tax reasons. Most of them are either retired or looking forward to retirement, and want to get back to the land. Most of them have a real liking for the land and a respect for farming. Nearly all of them admire and cherish their woodland. They all help to keep precious farmland out of the hands of speculators and developers.

Few New Englanders go hungry today, though their diet is quite different from that of three and a half centuries ago. Nobody that I know even tries to live on venison or roast woodchuck, hominy, fresh shad, boiled dock and milkweed and beet tops, thick bean soup flavored with pumpkin molasses, dried blackberries in Indian meal pudding, washed down with hard cider or peach brandy. From time to time, we have had venison in the freezer, fresh cod in the refrigerator, boiled dock and beet tops and lambsquarter, beef stew, baked beans (mine lightly flavored with vinegar), fresh-picked raspberries or blackberries, and a liqueur to go with the dessert, which may be pumpkin pie, mincemeat pie, or a rich, custardy bread pudding. But that's about the extent of our going native in the kitchen. It's more than most, I might add. And much of the time we settle for the standard American menu, which a great many other New Englanders grew up eating—bread and butter, meat and potatoes, with some kind of vegetable and dessert, take your pick.

59

60

62

63

CHAPTER 9

I BELIEVE I MENTIONED ELSEWHERE that not all New Englanders are laconic, nor are they all old-line Yankees. If anyone doubts this, I suggest he or she attend a New England town meeting. There one can see and hear a good cross-section of today's New Englanders and, if the topic of discussion rouses debate, one has ample proof that the Yankee can deliver quite a speech, and in vigorous language.

But before we go any further let me try to explain town meeting. It is basic to local government, even to democracy itself. The idea originated in New England and it persists here, where the town or township is the smallest organized geographical unit. (In the West, a township is simply a unit of land measurement, six miles square, and has no local government.) The New England township has no predetermined size. It may contain several villages, but all are governed by the township's three selectmen, who are chosen by secret ballot. Other town officials, from tax collector to fire warden, serve under the selectmen.

There is an annual town meeting, to hear and approve or disapprove reports of action taken and proposed. Special town meetings are called from time to time to discuss and advise on current questions. All residents of the township who are qualified to vote in state elections may vote at town meetings. Anyone may attend, but only qualified voters may have their say from the floor. Outsiders may speak if invited to do so by the moderator, who is chairman of the meeting. The moderator is not one of the town officials, hence is presumably impartial. He, or she, knows the rule book and can handle a heated debate.

It is there, as I was saying, that the Yankee tradition is sometimes broken by speeches ten or fifteen minutes long. Speeches by residents, not officials. The moderator usually curbs long-winded officials, but he tends to let voters have their say.

Outside town meeting there are exceptions, of course, who do their best to perpetuate the tradition. Such as the man who filled out a questionnaire about tobacco. Did he smoke (1) cigars, (2) cigarettes, (3) a pipe? His answer: "No." Did he use chewing tobacco? "Once." Did he stop? "Yes." Why? His answer: "No place to spit."

On the street in the village one Sunday morning, Barbara and I saw a couple probably in their sixties, in Sunday clothes and grim faces. He walked a couple of steps ahead of her, and she apparently had been talking at some length. But as we came within hearing she summed it up in seven words: "You're so hard to get along with!" He paused, she took his arm, and they went into the church together.

One old-timer, asked his ideas about today's relaxed rules, said, "You want my opinion about immorality, I'm ag'in it."

In the old days, when business on Sunday was forbidden, and people went to church in horse-drawn buggies, Yankee horse traders meeting in the churchyard would say, "If it was Monday, would you swap, even up?" And the answer: "If it was Monday, I'd say it'll take ten dollars to boot to make the trade."

I used to think the expression *ay-ah*, when used for *yes*, was either strictly Maine, where I first heard it, or back-country. Then I heard a well-educated physician from the Boston area use it, and after that a government official. But it still catches my ear.

Discussing the year's corn crop one autumn day, my neighbor said, "When I was a boy we put corn into sows and husked it out later."

"Sows?" I asked.

"Yes. Bundles, shocks. We called them sows."

To me, a sow was a female hog. But finally I ran it down in the unabridged Webster, where it is listed as Scottish or dialectical English for a stack or a heap. And I found that it is recognized as an old New England word, too. It probably went out with the invention of the corn picker and the silage chopper.

When we first came here, another neighbor spoke of a barway. It baffled me, until I saw that he meant what I had always called gate. But his word for it was logical. Most of the gates, as I called them, were closed by long cedar poles, or bars, slipped into slots in the posts on each side. I had half a dozen barways on my place, and now they are barways even to me. But the gate to the garden is still a gate. It has hinges.

Another baffler was *sluice*, sometimes lengthened to *sluiceway*. A sluice is what I used to know as a culvert. It is a pipe to carry water, rainwater or brook, from one side of a road to the other. And *brook* is another regional word, though no longer limited to New England. In the West a brook is a creek, and in the South it is a run. In many parts of the Midwest, however, a small stream is a brook, just as it is here and for the simple reason that most of the early settlers in Ohio, Indiana, and Illinois went there from Connecticut and Massachusetts. They took the word with them. But in the mountain West, where a creek is definitely a creek, fly fishermen never catch "creek trout." They catch brook trout, or brookies. Which indicates who caught those trout first—New Englanders, of course.

Talking with a townsman the other day, I heard him say, "We sent a truck to draw a load of sand." I constantly hear the word *draw* in this meaning among farm folk, a meaning for which I instinctively would use *haul*. But *draw* is one of the old words, deeply embedded in these New England hills. It goes all the way back to England and even has a root in Latin. I like it, though it still comes unfamiliarly to my tongue.

Popple is another native word with a fine old ancestry. The first summer I lived here a man spoke of the row of sugar maples on our land and said, "How do you suppose that maverick got in the row, that popple?" I had to smile, for in one sentence he had used a cow country word, *maverick,* and an old New England name for the poplar tree. He was right on both counts. That popple, a towering poplar, is a maverick in that row of maples. Now it and all the other poplars on this place are popples in casual conversation.

I hear the word *piney* only occasionally, but it is a good old word with Massachusetts roots. We have a whole row of pineys, which more pretentious gardeners call peonies, at the back of the perennial garden. *Piney,* however, is not a strange word to me. My Nebraska grandmother used it. We often smiled at the word, thought it was quaint and old-fashioned. But I learned, after my grandmother died, that she was right. The name comes from a Latin word, *paeonia,* which is much closer to piney than to peony. Grandmother came by the word honestly, for she had a grandmother from Massachusetts.

My Barbara insists that the nuts borne by hickory trees are walnuts. She admits that the trees are hickories, but says the proper name for the nuts is walnuts, at least here in Connecticut. For years I have tried to reason with her about it. No luck. Then, just the other day, poking into obscure references, I found this sentence: "Where the soil is somewhat poorer and drier, the commonest trees are black and white oaks and hickory, which early records call 'walnut.'"

The regional words dim out, which is too bad. Radio and television have done them in, I suspect. Even in regional skits, the words and accents are exaggerations and travesties. Those regional words were good words, most of them, colorful words. I hate to see them go. In fact, I intend to bundle the sweet corn stalks next fall into a sow, and tell all comers it *is* a sow. But I refuse to call a hickory nut a walnut.

Regional architecture is something else, as we say. Our farm lies in the borderland between the separate-buildings area and the all-under-one-roof area. North of here you begin to see the farm buildings set in a row and connected so the farmer can go to the woodshed, the privy, the wagonshed, and the barn without actually going outdoors in the worst of winter weather. The buildings are all under connecting roofs, though with differing roof levels. I have often wished our farm's buildings were arranged that way. North of here, too, the corn cribs have longer legs, stand higher off the ground. And here is another regional word: What I call a corn crib is locally called a *corn house*. The corn houses, or cribs, have longer legs because the winter snow usually is deeper.

And speaking of snow, there is no such thing as average snowfall in New England. Near the coast of Connecticut and Massachusetts they seldom get lasting snow before Christmas, and by mid-March the weather has turned springlike. Most snowstorms there, even in January, end in rain or, more unfortunately, sleet. They seldom get enough snow to protect the soil and garden plants from frost-heave.

Up north, however, in northern Vermont and New Hampshire and the upper part of Maine, winter usually is long, cold, and full of snow, which often covers the ground from Thanksgiving till mid-April. During this span, about eight feet of snow usually falls. At Vanceboro, Maine, one four-day snowstorm left eight feet of snow in one uninterrupted fall. January temperatures average below 10 degrees and nights often see 30 degrees below zero. The January thaw helps to ease things, but it never lasts more than a few days.

Here in the hills we are about halfway between the two extremes. We often have two feet of snow on the ground in January or February, but the January thaw usually takes it all off and we start fresh with an end-of-January storm. But by mid-March we usually have definite signs of spring. The year I write this, we had pussy willows out on March 8. Traditionally, maple sap begins to flow by Washington's birthday. Sugar-making begins, most years, by the first of March. I have seen the temperature here down to 26 below zero in January, but that is extreme. Ten below is the lowest it gets most winters.

New England's place names echo her people and her past, her Indian heritage and her native wildlife. We have lived with those names so long we often forget their origins, but as we read them we sometimes hear the music in their syllables.

New England, as an area, was first called that by England's Prince Charles, after he received a report from Captain John Smith in 1615.

Connecticut's name comes from Mohican words meaning "long river place."

Massachusetts got its name from Indian words meaning "large hill place," originally referring to present-day Milton, Massachusetts.

Maine was named for an old French province of the same name.

New Hampshire got its name from a county in England.

Rhode Island was first called Roode Eylandt for its red soil, by Adriaen Block, a Dutch explorer. Roger Williams' settlement there was called Providence Plantation. So in due time that tiny state adopted the resounding title, State of Rhode Island and Providence Plantation.

Vermont's name comes from the French for "green mountains," and her mountains were first called that by Samuel de Champlain.

For colorful names, though, look to the streams of this area. The river names practically sing: Penobscot and Kennebec, Housatonic and Androscoggin, Connecticut and Merrimac and Allagash. Indian names, every one of them. Try Chocorua and Mascoma and Pemigewasset. Try Shepaug and Missiquoit, Passumpsic and Walloomsac.

Some were named for remembered streams in England: Deerfield, Westfield, Farmington, Taunton, Thames—and don't call it Tems, English fashion; our Thames is pronounced to rhyme with James.

Keep remembering, or listening. There are countless Beaver Brooks and Roaring Forks. There are Sandy, Little, Great, Grassy, Stony, even Muddy Brooks. There are Goose Brook and Brant Brook, and Coon, Fox, Moose, Otter, Badger, Bobcat, and Mink Brook or Pond.

People? All kinds of people, from all over the world. But let's look at the ones who have rated headlines.

Of the thirty-eight men who have been President of the United States, six were born in New England. John Adams and John Quincy Adams and John Kennedy were Massachusetts natives. Franklin Pierce was born in New Hampshire. Chester A. Arthur and Calvin Coolidge were Vermonters.

Something in the soil, the air, maybe the climate, seems to have nourished the creative forces of outlanders as well as natives. That good gray triumvirate, Lowell, Longfellow, and Whittier, were natives. But Rudyard Kipling—a Yankee-in-law, by the way—came and spent four years in Vermont, and wrote his Jungle Books here, and *Kim* and *Captains Courageous*. Emily Dickinson and Edna St. Vincent Millay, strangely similar in poetic thought, quite different as persons, were natives. Robert Frost, an outlander, became the very voice of New England.

Noah Webster compiled his dictionary here. Harriet Beecher Stowe wrote her novel about Eliza and Uncle Tom. Mary Mapes Dodge and Kate Douglas Wiggin wrote their memorable children's stories. Mary Baker Eddy founded a church. Elias Howe invented the sewing machine. Samuel F. B. Morse invented the telegraph. Daniel Chester French, Gilbert Stuart, Augustus Saint-Gaudens painted and sculpted. Horace Greeley, Dorothy Canfield, George M. Cohan, Clara Barton—Yankees, every one of them, and doers, creators.

And as for people, just people, there are all those Irish and Italians and Portuguese and Poles, those Jews and Catholics and agnostics, who came here to work in the factories and intermarried with their Yankee neighbors and added new blood and strength as well as new names to the old stock.

And now let's get back to the land. To maple syrup, since I write this in the springtime. Maple syrup and maple sugar have been a luxury product of New England, particularly of Vermont, for a long time. Don't shout it from the housetops, but New York and Ohio also make such maple products, now and then more than all New England. No matter, the words *Vermont* and *maple syrup* still come together as automatically to the tongue as *ham and eggs*.

The Indians knew about making maple syrup, but they lacked good kettles in which to boil the sap. The whites had such kettles, and for quite a while "tree sugar" was easier to get and cheaper than white sugar, especially in the back-country.

Sugar and syrup-making continue, though not on the scale of fifty or seventy-five years ago. To make maple sugar, you need sugar maple trees. It takes forty years to grow a tree big enough to tap. A tap is a spile or spout set in a hole drilled two inches into the tree, and a sap bucket is hung from the spile. One tap is all the sap-gatherer puts in a tree with a twelve-inch trunk. A trunk twice that diameter or more can take four. The sap does not flow. It drips. It must be collected and boiled down to make syrup or sugar. It takes 35 to 40 gallons of sap to make one gallon of good syrup. Where wood is used for fuel under the shallow evaporator pans, a common rule is that a cord of wood is needed to boil down 875 gallons of sap into 25 gallons of syrup. The sap run ends when the leaf buds begin to swell.

Incidentally, Thomas Jefferson tried to grow productive sugar maples in Virginia. The trees grew very well indeed, but they didn't produce the same sugary sap they do in New England, and Jefferson never was able to make syrup from his maples.

One of the newest farm crops in New England is potatoes. Maine potatoes are known all over the country. Most of them come from Aroostook County, far up in northern Maine, which is one of the most recently settled areas in the East. When Henry Thoreau went there on a canoe trip in 1853 it still was frontier country. Central Maine was being logged for the first time and farmers coming in expected to grow wheat. They soon found that the soil and climate were ideal for huge crops of potatoes, and from the 1880s to the present, the potato crop in Maine has steadily increased.

The potato country is a beautiful tract with relatively few and far-apart towns, blue mountains in the distance, and dark forests all around. It is a land of gently rolling hills, but it lacks the snug feeling of most other parts of New England. And it seems totally alien to the coast of Maine, with its seafaring traditions and its Down East inflections. One of the early nineteenth-century observers speaks of an exceptional sea captain he met in Maine who was "devoid of the rawboned angularity which characterizes most of them and speaks very good English, through his mouth instead of his nose, quite an unusual circumstance."

That Maine inflection is beyond my power of description. I have heard it called "a rich Yankee twang," but that broad definition can apply all the way down to the Connecticut shore. The Maine sound is quite different, for instance, from the Boston or Harvard inflections, both of which now are often hard to find in their pure old state. The Harvard inflection too often has been perverted into a kind of bastard British accent with the *a*'s broadened, the *r*'s eliminated, and final *a*'s usually gulped into something like an "ugh." Hah-vuhd accent, in a word.

Lower New England, and much of the middle area, thanks to immigration from the hodgepodge cities, now speaks what has to be called "standard American," the language of the Midwest and West, sometimes with just a touch of the South. Diluted, of course, and emulsified with a variety of radio and television accents. Probably in time the old Yankee speech will totally disappear, and another item in the American heritage will be lost.

I have here on my desk a compilation of early laws and orders of the General Court of Connecticut which not only shows how completely the church dominated civil government, but is an excellent example of the language of the seventeenth century, and the customs and beliefs. For instance, it says at one point, "every person of the age of discretion, which is accounted fourteene yeares." In various places it speaks of "the clarke," meaning an official we now call clerk. In the phonetic spelling of the day, soldier was spelled "souldger" and sergeant was spelled "serjeant." Help was ordered for "pore persons," "earable ground" was taxable at such-and-such a rate, a "kysse" was a kiss and forbidden on Sunday. A chest is spelled "chist." A conspiracy was "a conspericie." The spelling here is indicative of the pronunciations of the day, since spelling was more or less phonetic at that time.

As far as the customs and codes of that day go, there was little leniency. "If any Childe or Children above sixteen years old and of sufficient understanding, shall curse or smite their naturall father or mother, hee or they shall be put to death." For theft, a man was to be whipped, have his ears cut off, be put to death. All cattle and swine had to be branded and ear-marked. And there is this provision: "If any man commit fornication, with any single woman, they shall be punished, either by injoyning in marriage, or fyne, or corporall punishment."

It all seems long ago and far away, but there it is, embedded in the soil and atmosphere, the very blood, of New England. You go to Hartford and you hear as many Spanish accents, from the Puerto Rican influx, as you do Yankee talk. You go to Boston and the Irish words, if not the accent, equal or outnumber the Yankee words. I go to nearby Canaan village and half the names, it seems, are Italian; some of those Italian-stock people are as Yankee as some whose families have been here two hundred years. When we go to Cape Cod, if it is any time except the "season" when the place is jammed with strangers, we find the old-stock Portuguese as numerous as the old-stock Yankees.

How can anyone make flat statements about such a people? As I suggested to start with, go to a town meeting and watch and listen. There you will see and hear New England.

65

66

69

CHAPTER 10

NEW ENGLAND is—how shall I say it—the parent of a dozen divergent colonies that, added up, became a nation of fifty states. Something of New England went into all of them eventually, for good or bad. Tenacity, as in the Revolutionary War leaders. Bigotry, as in the religious zealots. Love of the land—which did not always mean respect for the land. Industry and thrift and tight-fisted, private saving. Public improvidence and waste, particularly of natural resources. Pride and independence and self-sufficiency, which have been eroded from time to time by national and international economic problems.

International trade began here. Remember the Yankee sea captains and the clipper ships? Industry and the production line began here. Remember the household looms, the fireside tinkering and wood carving, and those water wheels in the brooks, powering the first few mills? The Revolution grew from Yankee discontent and rebellion. Remember Sam Adams and Tom Paine and the Tea Party and Bunker Hill? Slavery was abetted here. Remember the Indian captives sold to planters in Bermuda? The slave trade with Africa? Freedom for slaves became a crusade here. Remember the Underground Railroad and *Uncle Tom's Cabin* and mad old John Brown?

Innovation and dissent, in town meeting, in colonial council, in state legislature. An almost constant turmoil. Here in Connecticut, they are still debating the Blue Laws, which date back to early colonial days when Sunday was a church-mandated day and commercial dealing was a legal offense.

It is a strangely contradictory region, and yet the contradictions are not too difficult to live with. Man himself is a contradictory creature, tough and tender, wise and stupid, given to laughter and to tears. Even in its climate New England is contradictory. One of the toughest jobs I can imagine is that of a weather forecaster here. It is hard enough to guess what is happening meteorologically only five miles from here right now. The sun is shining here and it is a mild March day, but the sky may be dark and dreary over a cabin on Twin Lakes, just beyond the mountain behind our farmhouse.

A woman who once worked for us lives on a farm ten miles in the other direction, and her weather reports were pure Yankee. If we had an inch of snow, she said she had snow "right up to the calf's belly." If we had a scum of ice at the edge of the river, her brook was frozen "right down into the gravel." When the frost went out of the ground, she planted peas "in mud up to my knees."

She was a bit of Yankee contradiction herself. With an invalid husband and frail, elderly parents, she decided to "work out" to help make ends meet. For a time she worked as nursemaid for a business couple's young son, then as maid-of-all-work for us. Then one day, on the street in the village, the head of the local bank with whom she had been a classmate in high school said, "I need another teller. You always were good at math. Want to come in and work for me?" She said, "If I don't rob you broke, I'll break the bank with my mistakes within a year. I'll start work next Monday morning." So she put away her sneakers and dungarees, put on a dress, and went to work at the bank. At home, on the farm, she went right on milking her two cows and planting peas "in mud up to my knees." The bank, I probably need not add, is still solvent.

Inconsistent? No. Just Yankee.

Friends of ours who live in the ancestral house that once was a station on the Underground Railroad showed me a family account book from the 1870s, the years just after the Civil War. The figures were interesting, but I was fascinated by the story the account book indicated of a girl who became the family's maid-of-all-work and lived with them all her life. Our friend supplemented the figures with his own memories.

The girl went to work for them, in effect an indentured servant, at the age of twelve. After the first six months, she was paid 50¢ a week. From this was deducted the cost of cloth for her dresses, which she made for herself. When she was eighteen, she and the outdoor man, who cared for grounds and stable, were married. As a wedding gift, the family paid half the cost of the material for her wedding dress, debited the rest against her wages, which then were $1.25 a week. The total cost of the material was just under $10.

And that reminds me of the story a doctor in the village told me about the wife of an old-line Yankee farmer. The doctor came here fresh out of medical school and, among others, took care of the old-liner's family night and day, making house calls for croup and sciatica, indigestion and rheumatics. They admired him, did their best to pay his bills on time. After five years he told them he was getting married, and they told him they wished him happiness. The Missus showed him a bedspread she had just made, and when he admired it properly she said she'd like to make another like it for a wedding gift. Which she did. And then billed him for the cost of the material.

Characters, you say. Odd-balls. Maybe, and yet I wonder if they aren't honest people doing openly things that many of us would like to do, or do covertly.

Yankees. New Englanders. Sometimes they are amused at themselves, in their Yankee way of doing things. My neighbor who uses our pastureland for his dairy cows told me last fall, "The cows won't be up any more till spring. Getting too late to graze them. I told them, but just to make sure they understood, I put up a couple of poles in the barway." He always puts the cows out on the grass on May 10, regardless of the season. Some years the grass is almost knee-high by then. One such year I asked him why he didn't let the cows graze on it earlier, why May 10 had to be the date. "That," he said calmly, "is the day you put cows out on the grass." "The day your father did?" I asked. "And your grandfather, maybe?" And he said, "Probably. All I know is you put out the cows on May 10." And that closed the subject.

We have lived here almost twenty-five years. This is home. This is where our instincts turn for reassurance, for the continuity that gives our lives meaning. Perhaps if our parents and grandparents had cleared and plowed these acres, cut the lumber for this house, they would have more meaning, but I doubt it. Our great-greats from away back were part of this original colony, no matter where they came from and when. Or this colony was a part of them. Barbara's forebears were among the early settlers at Salem and Boston, back in the days of Naumkeag and Winthrop the elder and Roger Conant. On one side of my family, the early ones came soon after that, and were in the first movement west, to the Ohio Country. On the other side, they came somewhat later, with a wave of Scotch-Irish rebels who after the Revolution kept working westward, acre by acre and clearing by clearing, all the way to the Great Plains eventually. But with this Yankee ethos somewhere in their blood, this venture-and-retreat, this dare-and-deny, this go-and-stay-home factor throbbing in their arteries.

Thomas Wolfe said you can't go home again, and for his purpose he was right. But otherwise there is no truth in the statement. You can go back. We have come home, here. Not again, perhaps, but certainly home to where the roots were years ago, where the beginnings are.

New England is the homeland for a great many of us, whether we are tenth generation here or second generation. It is a land of people, once a land of trees. Mature, climax forest from the mouth of the St. Lawrence to the mouth of the Hudson, from the Atlantic to Lake Champlain. Then a land of hillside farms and stone walls and stony upland pastures. Then a land of abandoned farms and the trees creeping back, the persistent trees.

And a land of weather. In a total area about two-thirds as big as Colorado, a climate varying from that of Labrador to that of Virginia. And changeable as the wind. "If you don't like New England weather, wait a minute." Or, "We have two seasons, nine months of fall and winter, three months of rough sledding." I happen to live in a more temperate part, and in a river valley to boot, which gives the weather a degree of stability. We average between three and four inches of precipitation a month, and we have no dry season. Even so, here in Connecticut, we have about as many clear days as they do in the Deep South. About one day in three here is bright and sunny. In northern Vermont and New Hampshire and Maine, they have fewer sunny days. But we do have fog, even on sunny days, especially in late spring and early fall.

Summer temperatures seldom reach high into the nineties, which, we are told reassuringly, means ours are like summer temperatures in the lower Colorado mountains. True enough, as far as the thermometer goes. But there is also a hygrometer, which measures the humidity. With New England's normally higher humidity, 90 degrees is more like 105 in Colorado's dry air. Up here in our Berkshire hills, however, we usually have cool summer evenings. So cool that an elderly native told Barbara when we moved here not to put away her winter clothes in May. "You'll need a wrap and you'll welcome a warm dress from time to time all summer long."

And we have hurricanes, now and then. This is no new phenomenon. A vicious one swept New England in 1635, though it was not called a hurricane: It was merely "a severe wind storm and torrential rain." Another in 1815 tore things up a bit. About once in five to ten years, a storm of hurricane type gets up here in late summer or early fall. The one in 1938 was vicious. So was the one in 1955. Such storms strike New England with particular intensity because they come up the coast, over the ocean, gaining force all the way from the West Indies. New England lies broadside to their path, with the eastward-jutting coast of Connecticut and Massachusetts. With that coastal area thickly settled, the wind and water batter and inundate homes and harbors, factories and farmland, as well as surging up the rivers and creating havoc inland.

But such outbursts are exceptional. Most autumns are relatively calm, leading to Indian summer intervals that are unequaled elsewhere. Long autumns, usually, followed by frost and moderate snow around Christmas.

Abroad they smile at us when we speak of being "an old land," but in comparative terms New England *is* old. Not old in the English sense, with Roman occupation before the Christian era, but with Indian occupation equally old. The ancestors of the Indians were here when Stone Age people were scribing pictures of bison on the walls of caves in Europe. The old habit of thinking that history began here only with the arrival of Europeans is understandably egocentric. But in our own terms, our own comparatives, New England is old.

When we first came here I asked who built those stone walls that mark forgotten fields on our mountainside. Nobody living here-about could say. The great-great-grandfathers built them, and the great-great-grandsons are now in Illinois and Texas and Iwo Jima. That's one thing that happened to the land. The generations moved away. And now it seems incredible that those who gathered stones from the fields, stone-boated them to the line, and laid them in dry-wall patterns that still stand—incredible that they had time to do other things besides. They built their houses and their barns, they plowed and planted and reaped, they tended their sheep and their cattle and saw that their families were provided for. And now even their names are forgotten. But the walls are still there, miles and miles of stone walls all over New England, writing their anonymous story of the past.

Maybe one should say the trees and the stones, maybe even the climate, made strong men of them. Tested them, and got rid of those who didn't shape up. Or is that too severe a judgment? I am only speculating, wondering.

And how much has man shaped the land? He has cut the trees, repeatedly, and each time they have grown back. Not the same trees, not such big trees, but trees, woodland cover for the land. The trees on our own mountainside are not commercially important. They would mostly rate only as pulpwood, I suppose. And that is true of far too many New England acres. But at least they cover the rocks and soil, prevent more erosion. Those woodlands have already housed several generations, barned and stabled their livestock, fueled their fires. They have smelted the ore that made plowshares and cannon, pocket knives and bayonets, nails and ox shoes, and kettles to render the oil from whale blubber. They have made bags for groceries and paper for books and webs to flow through the thundering presses and emerge as tomorrow morning's newspaper.

When he had cut the trees, man created fields and pastures where the trees had grown. And for a few years, less than a man's lifetime in most places, the fertility and the soil remained. Then the rain and the endless plowing let the land seep away in dirty runnels, and the barren hillsides became blueberry patches and brushy tangles. And when a thin layer of humus had accumulated, the trees came back to claim the hills again, the insistent trees.

Man dug the ore, and made a pit where there had been a hill. He hauled the sand and gravel—pardon the outlander's tongue—with his teams and trucks he *drew* the sand and gravel from the beds where the glaciers left it, built roads and bridges and concrete walls. And left the gaping pits like open gashes on the land. And eventually the grass and brush tried to heal the scars.

Man filled the marshes and killed the salt hay, which had fed the cattle and protected the garden from the winter cold. He cut down the hills and filled the valleys, "to make more usable land." He cut roadway lanes through the woodland "to get there faster."

People, then, shaped the land to their own notion of what a land should be. Not always and not everywhere; but you can't put twelve million people on sixty-seven thousand square miles of land and expect the land to be unchanged. Roads and superhighways have been spread from border to border. Lanes for power transmission lines have been slashed through the woodland. Streams have been dammed, ponds and lakes have been polluted and aged before their time.

But the land persists, and the trees, as I seem to have said over and over, perhaps because the trees somehow signify the integrity of life and growth.

The land persists, and something in the human heart and emotions, perhaps in a kind of race memory, responds. I doubt that it is only because New England is near at hand, but urbanites come here at all seasons, to look again at trees and hills and brooks, to reassure themselves, perhaps, that such realities still exist. Older people, who have made their competence elsewhere, come and buy property that they may hold a share of this land, may live here now or later and belatedly be a part of the old simplicities. Young people come, scorning the conventions and the whole life pattern of the cities, to "get back to nature." Some fumble, total strangers that they are to the land, and keep reaching for another way of life, trying to get back to safe beginnings. Some of them, like some of their well-off elders who came also seeking, fail to see or understand what they find, and give up, go back to their own cultural ghettos. But others stay and live the whole experience, from colonial hardship to self-sufficiency, independence, and triumph. They are, for the most part, an earnest, practical generation and may yet have worthwhile things to tell us, once they have learned the fundamentals.

Typical of those I am thinking about is a young couple who wearied of what seemed a pointless rat race here in southern New England. Both had jobs, they had two small children, they owned an equity in their house. But they wanted something more. They went to Maine, found and bought a tract of woodland in a loose-knit colony of back-to-the-land young folk. He built a log cabin there from plans he found in a book, while she returned to her job until their house was sold. Then she and the children joined him in the new venture, practically starting from scratch. "This," she said, "is what we want to do. For now, anyway, Maybe this way we can find what life is all about. We never could, going on the way we were."

A few years ago we had the flower children, who occasionally came up this way looking for something, too, which I never could identify. I tried to talk to one group of them I met along our back-country road. They had packs on their backs, were barefoot "to feel the earth," wore wilted daisies and black-eyed Susans in their long hair. "It doesn't matter what we're looking for," a spokesman for the group said. "It's the search, the Pilgrimage, that counts. The Pilgrimage, whether there is a Promised Land or not." And one sad-eyed girl—nobody in the group was as happy as I had expected them to be—handed me a wilted daisy and, with a wan smile, gave me her whispered benediction, "Peace." But they didn't stay. The next afternoon my friend at the filling station over on the main highway said they stopped at his place that morning, cold and hungry, and began hitching rides back toward New York.

I'm sorry they didn't find what they were looking for, but as their spokesman said, "It's the search that counts." Actually, that has been true of New Englanders for a long, long time. They came here searching. They were fanatic about it, true enough; they denied others that same right to search along different paths. But it has been the search that mattered for all these years, and it still seems to be. We came here searching and we found that most of those already here, even the ones with long lines of Yankee forebears, were searching. And most of those who come here today are searching. Not all for the same thing, of course. But hoping to find some degree of peace with themselves and the world, if nothing else.

That is not unique to any people or any place. Man is a perverse creature. He believes in freedom, yet can be savagely intolerant. He may worship a wise and merciful God, yet he can be barbarously cruel to his own kind. Remember the witch hunts in Salem in the 1690s and the 19 women who were hanged. But don't forget, if you ever heard, that in 1864 Colonel John Chivington, once presiding elder of the Methodist Conference for Nebraska and Kansas, led an armed force that killed more than 400 Indians, most of them women and children, near Fort Lyons, Colorado. What were they searching for, those witch-hunters and those Indian-killers? Peace with themselves? . . . But forget that unenlightened past and its excesses. This is today and, God help us, we are still looking for peace and a roof and three meals a day. Once we are assured of those, we can provide the rest, if we can only salvage a woodland, a clean-running river, and a few acres of farmland.

So the outlanders, and many of the natives who have become immured in the cities, come here to find reassurance. They don't call it that. They call it recreation, not stopping to think that recreation is, basically, creation again, renewal of the fundamentals. They come to ski, at almost countless skiing centers from northwestern Connecticut to northern Vermont and New Hampshire. They come to climb and hike, some along the Appalachian Trail, which starts southward from Mount Katahdin in Maine, and some finding their own trails in the Taconics, the White Mountains, or the Greens. Many come to fish, along with the countless fishermen who live here, in brooks and lakes, the inland waters that once were alive with trout and bass and, in special places, salmon and shad, and many of which are stocked annually to continue the fiction of clean streams and endless plenty. Many come for the summer, especially to these New England hills and mountain areas where the combination of altitude and green grass and trees creates what used to be called a salubrious climate. Some come to swim, to bathe, to sail small boats, to merely sit and watch the summer clouds and hear the birds.

I've said that people come to New England for reassurance, but that probably is grandiloquence, even bombast. Who, after all, needs reassurance? And please don't waken at two o'clock in the morning and telephone me to tell me we all do. I know that, but I see no need to trumpet it. Let's just say that we don't *need* New England for that; or let's say you can find that anywhere you really look.

150

But New England is handy, nearby for many people. It is not yet wholly urbanized; there are reminders of what it, and all this country for that matter, used to be. The region is no longer a wilderness. It hasn't been for a long, long time, in terms of human life. New England is no longer a religious enclave, though many of the strictures and much of the idealism, as well as the formalism, of religious rule persist. In government, that is, though not always, or even often, in personal conduct. The born Yankee is fundamentally an independent person, shrewd and prudent, competent and diligent, not one to overlook opportunity when it appears.

New England has been a warehouse of timber and iron ore, of seafood and whale oil, of far-ranging ships and ship masters. It has used them, and used them well. It has created culture, and music, and literature, and retailed them to the world. It created forms of self-government and provided leaders who could dream—and scheme—with the best dreamers anywhere in the world.

What more can be asked for one small corner of such a nation as the United States of America?

71

73

LOCATIONS OF PHOTOGRAPHS

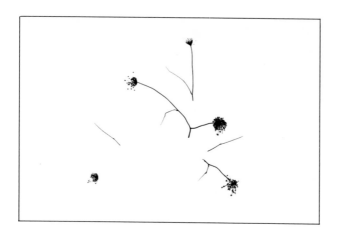

A PLACE TO BEGIN

was designed by Klaus Gemming, New Haven, Connecticut,
and printed in fine-screen duotone process
by George Rice and Sons, Los Angeles, California
on 80-lb. Lustro Offset Enamel dull coated paper,
manufactured by the S. D. Warren Company.
The text and the display lines were set in Linofilm Sabon
by Finn Typographic Service, Inc., Stamford, Connecticut.
The cover fabric is Milbank Linen
produced by the Columbia Mills, Inc.
The book was bound by A. Horowitz & Son, Fairfield, New Jersey
and its production was supervised by
David Charlsen, San Francisco, California.

SIERRA CLUB BOOKS